Dear Madame de Beauvoir

Daniel Zanou

Library of Congress Control Number: 2023920298
ISBN: Softcover   979-8-3694-1004-2
                     eBook   979-8-3694-1003-5

Print information available on the last page.

Rev. date: 10/20/2023

To order additional copies of this book, contact:
Xlibris
844-714-8691
www.Xlibris.com
Orders@Xlibris.com
856555

Contents

Preface

"Dear Madame de Beauvoir" responds to existentialist feminism. It exposes the flaws in radical feminism and provides essential tips for our daughters to navigate safely the world created by men. The world of men and women has reached an impasse; men accuse women, who, in turn, see men with unkind eyes. The scriptures recommend not to separate what God has joined together, but today, we barely believe that both individuals are designed to be together.

The book introduces essentialist feminism, a new school of thought within the feminism movement that sees man and woman as inseparable entities living in an obligatory symbiotic relationship. They are joint heirs and co-equal in managing the material universe. They have never been in war, as anarchist feminists tend to depict it, but in lovely relationships that sometimes do not end well because society has no cognizance of their constitutions.

Man and woman complete and complement each other; they can switch tasks in the house as they please, but roles cannot be abolished because we cannot have two captains in one boat. The two individuals live as a pilot and co-pilot and cannot leave the house simultaneously because the ship cannot be left unattended. Essentialist feminism advocates for being first before any doing and emphasizes the functional Information humans carry in their chromosomes. Therefore, it promotes function-based roles in the marital home to address the nascent confusion in marriages instead of the gender-based roles we traditionally practice.

By claiming equality, radical feminists have made it harder for women because they try to compare what is incomparable. Is there any way to compare a rotor and a stator? Both parts have meaning together, but separately, they are insignificant; so do man and woman. This book tackles equality-based programs and expects to replace them with an equity-based agenda.

"Dear Madame de Beauvoir" is a suggestion to help our daughters navigate the world of men; it is not a mandatory guide. It is a protection mechanism to assist young girls who are anxious about life in this modern society to escape the trap of aggressive men. Men are not monsters, though; they thrive in their roles, and we cannot deny their nature. The book comes to explain to our daughters why men behave the way they do and why new knowledge is necessary to cope with the situation. There is functional Information inside living organisms, and life unfolds accordingly, a phenomenon many psychologists and philosophers tend to mock. This fact changes everything.

Humans only see less than one percent of the entire spectrum, yet they believe all of existence is what they can see. How can we have an intellectual discussion with these people? A scientist mockingly said religious people read one book and barely finish it, yet think they know everything. Don't we have a similar phenomenon with scientists and philosophers? The electromagnetic spectrum yields less than one percent in visible light, and scientists believe that's all that exists. These two groups of people are the leaders of our planet; our world is divided between science and religion's rulership that refuses, unfortunately, to put some water in their wine. We remind them to reconsider their stances because they don't know everything; science and religion don't have the privilege of the truth. We are bold in our philosophy and science not because we are smart; we stand tall because religious people and scientists have made some errors in their approaches. Something is not adding up in their endeavors, and that's why the world is in turmoil. The scriptures said, "It is the glory of God to conceal a matter, but the glory of kings is to search out a matter." This verse means all humans are seekers on Earth because God is the King of kings; we are kings, therefore, seekers.

Humans are lying too much to themselves and their children; consequently, things are not working. People are suffering not because life is brutal but because they don't understand it. The youth is confused, and juvenescence has become an assault course full of anxiety. American adolescence is in a dire crisis. Meanwhile, consciousness has evolved, and human society is supposed to take off, but we are still lagging behind schedule; why? The answer is in our manufactured ideologies and doctrines. An American philosopher once said I quote:

"There's simply no polite way to tell people they've dedicated their lives to an illusion."

In this book, we summoned humans bluntly, speaking without taboos, calling things by their names as de Beauvoir did because we firmly believe the problem of humans is solvable. I don't want to sound arrogant and condescending, but the issue is even easier to solve than people might think. We shed tears not because our works are opposed but because society denies life to the young generation (we like critics and intellectual debates, though). The world is worrisome for everyone, but suffering in the West and US is unacceptable because their ancestors have labored to provide the necessary ingredients that the youth needs to make the life journey a happy event. All the resources are in place: natural, intellectual, and material, for the youth to have a decent and comfortable life as the Founding Fathers have promised. Why do the youngsters keep struggling? Why are they still anxious? I could understand an adult who commits suicide, but I am flummoxed to hear about a young individual who destroys his life in a society where a table is dressed up for him. The forefathers have dug the well; the job of the youngsters is to water the grass.

We try to open the eyes of radical feminists; the goal here is to be pragmatical to solve practical issues in our society. The moment is not to continue gaslighting society but to take advantage of the amendment to improve women's condition. Human society has improved, and we offer this book as a light on the path of our daughters to navigate the society humans have built. Men and women have built a society, and although women tend to exclude themselves from this "modern building," they have always been passive supporters of men's hegemony. The time has come for women to take responsibility, adjust their positions, and affirm their new functions.

"Dear Madame de Beauvoir" is a response to the book "The Second Sex" by the French philosopher Simone de Beauvoir. We sift through her philosophy to expose human society from a new perspective. At the beginning of the project, we wanted to write a laconic reply to the topic, but seeing the colossal work of Simone de Beauvoir, we shifted our position and decided to address the issue with a book; nobody can salute 978 pages with a dozen pages of a dissertation. We have to admit that de Beauvoir's work is a monument, and the author herself is an outstanding philosopher and an icon in the feminist movement. Thus, one must have guts to come against her; it was a bold project we undertook, and we remained more diffident all the way to the end. We use anachronism as a shield to move forward in our argumentation.

While de Beauvoir had an accusatory look at the world, we, on the contrary, look critically at human society and offer pragmatic solutions. We explain various trajectories of the life journey to our daughters so that the individual may know in advance the ending of her choice. Our sisters and mothers could regret their choices because they didn't know; our daughters will not have any excuses because they know better. Essentialist feminism reveals the true nature of human beings and the society we have built. We are philosophers, not activists, and we devise this line of thought based on the assumption that human beings are medium consciousness, therefore, separated from the animal kingdom. Essentialist feminism will work if only humans operate as creatures of love and not self-love; it is a program based on equity instead of equality.

Our philosophy often highlights the failure of parents, and we know people hate us for stressing that, but it is a fact; we don't make it up because everybody can observe this reality of our society. We believe parents' eyes will open to the problem if they let this remark percolate throughout their grey matter. We have devised pragmatic solutions to assist them in addressing the issue. Our assertions in this book are the fruit of more than 20 years of observations and experiments, and we possess whatever we advance.

However, the readers need to familiarize themselves with our particular writing styles. We are saying new things or dealing with topics science ditched in the past because scientists and philosophers judged them unreal or taboo. For that cause, we are generous and lavish in our explications, trying to explain what we mean in various ways possible to avoid the reader being confused; this particular method is common in our writings. Therefore, when reading this book, the reader must not stall on one statement; if the individual does not understand something, the chances are great we will repeat it elsewhere differently. The book deals with practical situations, so we make an effort to help the reader understand whatever we mean. The reader must also know that all comparisons in this book are made ceteris paribus, and most statistics deal with social science.

We are now well established in our philosophy and science, and we remind the readers to separate both disciplines. There is no way to tell people which idea is a philosophy and which one is related to science in writing. We differentiate the two fields through testing; anything that is reproducible and testable is science. Therefore, we require critical thinking as science responds regardless of individual belief systems. As one American science communicator said in his "Masterclass," we have to think critically to save the world. Let's do it; let's cast aside all tools and high-tech experiments that easily distract us from focusing on the reality before us. The founders of modern science established our knowledge through observation. I finish here on this pertinent question of the Turkish Nobel laureate, Orhan Pamuk:

"Why do people prefer lies to our scientific truths?"

Life Is Not Fair

It had been a great privilege and honor to sit at your table. I came to the banquet with the invitation card of my father. Five centuries earlier, René Descartes responded to the invitation of the Greek philosophers, and he disagreed with their teachings. He destroyed everything in the house. Like Jesus drove all merchants out of the temple, scattered the money changers' coins, and overturned their table, Descartes rejected the Aristotelian teachings that dominated Europe during the Renaissance.

I heard about your inquietudes about woman's questions, and I couldn't resist taking my pen to answer you. I was afraid of all these ladies at the table and didn't dare to raise my voice lest they accused me of mansplaining. Who am I to explain to women what belongs to woman? Do I have a womb? Do I possess breasts to breastfeed a child? How can I explain to a woman the feeling of suckling a baby? Could a man explain to a woman how it feels to carry a pregnancy?

Only a woman is qualified to explain how it feels to welcome a man inside her. But when you asked what a woman was, I had urticaria, my mouth itched, and I wanted to say something. I had a strong urge to answer your question. My father taught me well. He provided personally for my education and made me stand in the circle of great thinkers. I didn't talk at the dinner; I preferred to write to you.

When the scholar said a woman is a womb, some women disagreed, but I don't think he said something terrible. Frankly, a woman is a womb; yes, she is, and we must not deny it. Sometimes, how we look at circumstances and observe things causes prejudice; the interpretation we make of reality is often the problem in our society. As you genuinely pointed out in your magnum opus, "The Second Sex," the subjugation of women, the Jews, and the Blacks was appalling. But bear with me a moment, and let me reassure you that human society is changing. A young Nazi with blue eyes and blond hair was taught to look at an indigenous and perceived him as a lesser being. Since when does the level of hormones in the body systems make an individual lesser than a human being? Is a Spaniard lesser than a German? Is a Bedouin of Morocco inferior to a Spaniard? Is a Tuareg of Mali lesser than a Bedouin? And finally, is a Nilotic from Sudan low in the ranking compared to a Tuareg?

Is the world so designed, or are we dealing with human constructs? A woman is not lesser than a man; society makes it so. You and I share a lot in common; Nature has condemned us in perpetual battle until our oppressor comes to age and opens his eyes. Do we have other choices? Is there any other option? An atheist once told me the Earth is a prison, but I didn't believe him; I am a Christian. I am also a philosopher, and I learned that women, the Jews, the proletariat, the indigenous, and the Blacks must always be united when facing oppression. I love how you mainly chose the trio made of women, the Jews, and the Blacks to adumbrate tyranny and depict injustice in human society. The grind is real, but we must not lose hope because justice, love, and peace will prevail at the end.

Dear Madame de Beauvoir, I urge you not to consider several teachings of the Greeks on women; they got the female human wrong. They have led many astray because they apprehended the question outside reality; I speak with some diffidence. Aristotle had said such claptrap about women when he stated that we should regard women's nature as suffering natural defectiveness[1]. In Part V of Book one of "Politics," he stipulates that the male is superior by nature and the female inferior; I am still pondering how people manage to compare men and women to reach such a conclusion. I could understand the Greek philosopher, but when you mentioned that Saint Thomas also jumped into the puddle to take over and state that a woman is "an incomplete man, I was left totally flabbergasted; I didn't expect to hear such a twaddling declaration from a Church dignitary. Christian scholars are supposed to know better because Jesus appointed us as the world's light and salt. The master was not wrong when making such a bold statement because we receive a teacher when welcoming the Holy Spirit. We carry the light and know better, but stay with me; many of these scholars were wrong because they interpreted the scriptures with their human minds. Jesus requested his followers receive the Holy Spirit to assist them with the scriptures; it's a prerequisite to being a son of God. Unfortunately, many scoffed at his recommendation, and every Christian since then has made his own interpretation of the Book.

God indeed shows himself through the Bible as a man, and he often displays himself through a male character

---

[1] Simone de Beauvoir attacked Aristotle's point of view in the introduction of the first volume of her book "The Second Sex." She exposed how many European thinkers continued in the same line of thoughts as the Greek philosopher without pondering over the topic.

because the Holy Spirit is active. Without a doubt, a man is a dynamic force, as you noticed it; men operate with transcendence while women thrive by immanence, but both do complete and complement each other; there is no way we can compare them. I shall come back to this topic later.

Life is not fair; however, the woman is not second to man, and the African man is not at the bottom of humanity. In his Dakar address in 2007, President Sarkozy stated that the African man has not fully entered into history[2]. He forgot Egypt, Nubia, and Ethiopia. The Greeks, the Hebrews, and the Romans learned in Egypt; the source of modern knowledge comes from Egypt. Moreover, slavery is a thing because someone has to work to feed the aristocracy and their children so that they can have peace of mind to think correctly to reach an invention. Voltaire nicely put it in his masterpiece "Candide, ou L'optimisme," when narrating the misery of the maimed negro in chapter 19, I quote:

"When we labor in the sugar works, and the mill happens to snatch hold of a finger, they instantly chop off our hand; and when we attempt to run away, they cut off a leg. Both these cases have happened to me, and it is at this expense that you eat sugar in Europe."

An enslaved person needed to work on the plantation in Saint-Domingue to produce sugar so that Lavoisier could take his breakfast and notice that nothing is created in nature, nothing is lost, and everything changes. How could

---

[2] Ba, D. (2007) "Africans still seething over Sarkozy speech," Reuters; https://www.reuters.com/article/uk-africa-sarkozy/africans-still-seething-over-sarkozy-speech.

he reach such a conclusion if he was hungry? The adage says a hungry stomach has no ears. It took free labor to feed nations in Europe so that thinkers and scholars could think and reach their inventions. Unfortunately, the Europeans and their children often forget that.

In the same way men never counted women's achievements and support, the white man has no record of the black man's contribution. Moreover, he toiled to erase anything good he could hear from the black man to justify his absurd eugenics theory. The Africans must be devoid of humanity for social Darwinism and Eugenics to stand firmly. But nowadays, we are aware of how life has manifested itself on this planet. Nothing sprang up spontaneously on its own as materialist scientists tried to sell it to us; functional Information was behind every living organism on Earth.

As we know today, life manifests itself as a living existence in this material universe. That life, which religious people call Zoe, expresses itself through material objects. Zoe, the source of all things, materializes and distinguishes itself as males and females throughout the animal kingdom; these expressions are particular in humans and are known as man and woman. Indeed, a demarcation line separates humans from the rest of the animals.

God exists, although we are not ready to prove it scientifically. However, we can study his manifestation, and we know it is imperfect because of entropy. While life is symmetrical in the immaterial realm, its expression in the material world is asymmetric. That's why living organisms are halved down in males and females. One is not superior to another; they complete and complement each other. Sadly, human ideology and philosophy create a caste system with social classes. Inequality in human society emanates from failed philosophies and false doctrines. As I pointed out earlier, we are not less human because we have a higher pigmentation in our skin. A woman is not inferior to a man because she has a womb. The German philosopher Arthur Schopenhauer went further when he compared women to big children, an intermediate state between the child and the full-grown man[3]. It is outrageous how he lamentably failed in his analysis. I know one can be a great mind and miss the point. Schopenhauer crashed his mind on this topic. Look at how I tackled him. I devised a thought experiment to expose the great man.

My thought experiment goes that way. One day, all women fall dead, and men mourn their dead ones. Life goes on. Centuries later, the human species goes extinct. Men have no womb, and our technology cannot cultivate human babies. Humans disappear within two centuries following the cataclysm as they die in old age without offspring.

In the second simulation, it is men who fall dead. When women notice their losses, those among them who are physicians and surgeons cut open the scrotum of deceased men and collect their sperm. They fertilize some of the women who are in their ovulation windows. They give birth to several baby boys within a year. They take good care of

---

[3] The German philosopher was very rude to women throughout his essay "on Women." This particular dissertation could be found in his collections of essays online; Schopenhauer, A. (2004) "Essays of Schopenhauer," The Project Gutenberg Ebook of Essays.

these boys, who become able and strong men. After two centuries, the human species is still thriving.

In my thought experiment, it appears clearly between men and women who eventually hold the strategic position in the process of life. Our daughters must be careful with the false narration of superiority and inferiority; it is the trap men use against women. If feminists don't change their narrative, they will be like the poor Texan who sat broke on his land full of oil. Women perpetuate life, and they are the matrix through which the next generation is cooked. Destroy all women, and human life goes extinct. Men cannot do it without women; it is clear. It has always been a big lie to portray women as inferior and insignificant.

The human species comprises half of the women, and the remaining half sojourned in her womb. Women fabricate from scratch, out of her energy, the other half of the world population. They manufacture men; I can boldly say the first woman is a human being; for man, nobody really knows where he comes from. The Bible said he was made out of the dust of the ground; so be it. Women give life; that's a fact.

We must know and understand how life unfolds on earth. The manifestation of life is not perfect, and we must teach our children to get used to it. I am a black soul; that's what they said. Do I complain? No! You are a woman, and you must not make a drama out of it. Radical feminism is forcing women to be other things than a woman. Life is not fair. Until humanity wakes up from years of torpor, we are doomed.

Nonetheless, there is good news to celebrate: consciousness is growing up. Women, the Jews, and the Blacks need to be patient. Recently, we have discovered the information-bearing properties inside the human body, upending the science behind Darwinism; evolution is not random. We are progressing slowly but surely, and one day, the white man will wake up from his lethargy.

As Darwin purports in his work, life is a power struggle. Nobody wants to be at the bottom; unfortunately, the natural distribution seems to put some individuals at the bottom. We must accept it, not because people who dominate are correct but for harmony and peace. According to Frederic Saldmann, human existence spans over 120 years[4]. What a life will we offer our children if they spend all their existence fighting? If reincarnation exists, everything is balanced. Imagine Francisco Pizzaro, the Spanish conquistador who exterminated the Inca people, had already been reincarnated as an Indian buddy, had his head smashed by a British colonial soldier in Calcutta, and Pocahontas had lived as Napoleon. If so, wisdom is required among humans to avoid killing one's own children. What if people have been killing their siblings since then without knowing it? Who knows if Stalin has been reincarnated as a Ukrainian soldier? Could the Russian troops kill that soldier if they knew he was Stalin? Imagine George Washington reincarnated in Iraq when the American soldiers attacked the city. Could they still drop a bomb on that city, knowing that Washington

---

[4] Saldmann is a French physician of preventive medicine in Paris. He exposed some of his ideas in his popular Tedx talk in 2016. Saldmann, F. (2016) "Toute mort avant 120 ans est une mort prématurée » | Frederic Saldmann | TEDxMarseille: https://www.youtube.com/watch?v=KFxEcTolF4o&t=622s

was living there as a baby? The karmic concept has been debunked by the work of Jim Tucker; however, the individual seems to pass emotions, behaviors and some physical cues from one life to the other. Arthur Schopenhauer believed the Will is one, manifesting through every living organism as a Representation. Humanity is one; we are all brothers, and failure to understand it is causing much trouble on this planet. There is no man or woman, black or white, Jew or Muslim, Russian or Ukrainian, Hutu or Tutsi, South Korean or North Korean; a human being is what exists.

The Bible causes prejudice, at least in its interpretation, but be reassured; it has always been misinterpreted. Intelligent people see the flaws in the scriptures, and that's why they reject the Christian God, but they are wrong: God exists. The scriptures are the story of humans, not the story of God. It is a book that depicts the rebellion of humans, the secession of the material world from the immaterial realm from which derives the schism of living organisms into males and females. Humans alter the natural division to create a caste system. That's how we get men on top of women and, later, the Caucasian man on top of the entire human race. Shall we stand against the natural order? As an essentialist feminist and a man from Africa, I pray that the white man acquires wisdom to be a wise ruler. Someone must necessarily lead the world. A ship needs a captain, but woe unto the crew if the commander is foolish. You live in a period where the captain of the ship was a big fool, warring from dawn to dusk. He was such a moron that he sacrificed his children in a bloody war and destroyed his own cities and habitations. George Marshall, the United States Secretary of State, had to borrow a considerable amount of money to rebuild his residences. Today, our children continue to pay the interest on the loan. Unfortunately, they haven't learned anything from their mistakes and are about to reproduce them again. Indeed, the white man is not wise, but we have nobody to replace him. The world has simply a foolish ruler; that's the conclusion we have reached, and we must deal with it. The white man is about to start another world war again.

While the white man was a big fool in your epoch, he seems to wake up in my era, although still blurry, squinting to adjust his vision, and his mind starts connecting the dots of existence. Life will change if he becomes wise, but we cannot pull on the tree to make it grow; we need to be patient and give him enough time to figure it out by himself. Proverb 25:2 said:

"It is the glory of God to conceal a thing, but the honor of kings is to search out a matter."

The scriptures have made the white man err in his interpretations. When the Romans brought the Hebrew writings to Europe, the Caucasian man was so fascinated that he regretted God didn't commission him but chose a Jew. So, he took the words of the apostles Paul and Peter at heart. He assigned himself a mission to lead, teach, and guide the rest of humanity to the light. It is a noble job, except that the leadership of Jesus is clear: whoever wants to be great among you must be your servant. Did the European missionaries grab this statement?

I understand why you become an atheist. You grew up as a Roman Catholic believer like my father, Descartes, but you switched and became an atheist as your rational mind became operational. You are not alone; many intellectuals struggle with Christianity, but once again, God exists, although we are not ready to prove it. Human stupidity must not let us err and deny reality. If we observe Nature closely, we can see patterns and harmony everywhere.

Moreover, there is functional Information behind all living organisms, and anyone who fails to perceive such reality is still sleeping. The British philosopher Anthony Flew woke up and noticed how Nature is well woven. He knew the functional Information must have an author because a well-structured language cannot exist independently. One thing is to have a brain, and another is to use it.

Your companion said humans don't have any essence, a statement you admitted, which I disagree with in my philosophy. At some points, existence precedes essence, but essence does precede existence on many occasions. Unlike the Sartrean analogy of the paper-knife[5], which is designed exclusively to perform a specific role, humans, on the contrary, are free yet are also designed to perform a particular function because they carry a set of information that regulates their existence. The paper-knife is not free, and it can never do anything else except its primarily assigned role. But humans are free to choose; they have volition. They can perform against their original function. A man has the freedom to become whatever he wants to be.

---

[5] Sartre used this analogy in the public lecture he gave in Paris in October 1945 to clarify his existentialist vision developed in his 1943 book "Being and Nothingness." Notice that the year Sartre used this symbol, the mystery of the DNA molecules haven't been elucidated yet. Nobody knew functional Information was embedded inside the body of living organisms. Sartre, J. (1946) "L'Existentialisme est un Humanisme," Les Editions Nagel

He can be a farmer, a soldier, or a writer if he decides so. God does give us a purpose because his signature is inside us. God does not constrain us to follow the program he puts inside us because the individual is free to end his life at any time he wants. If God can coerce us to do against our Will, we will be unable to kill ourselves. The fact that the individual can kill himself proves that God does not coax us. We are free to follow his agenda or not. One thing is sure: if we follow the most dominant program inside our body, what we call gifts, we are fulfilled and satisfied. If we don't, we feel miserable, continually seeking approval from others. The program inside us makes us the boss of our own existence, and we seek nobody's support to be happy. We are fulfilled no matter what as long as we can deploy that innate program inside our DNA. We are free to deploy the program or not, and this fact causes human life to be divided between voluntarism and fatalism; that's my philosophy. I set my approach to human life at the crossroads between the essentialism of Plato and the existentialism of Sartre. The degree to which we operate in one or the other is determined by reincarnation, a doctrine science is not yet ready to confirm.

Plato believed in reincarnation; the Hebrew tradition also considered reincarnation until Christians suppressed the ideology in Europe. The idea was present and strewn throughout the entire scriptures; the Roman Catholic Church and Christian scholars started hiding it because it went against their doctrines and dogmas. Science sprouted out of the decadence of the Western Church, and scientists carried on in the same wake. Reincarnation is a fact, and we will find out sooner or later; it is just a matter of time. Notice that scientists killed Ignaz Semmelweis, the Hungarian physician who postulated the existence of germs. Today, every doctor washed their hands in hospitals and clinics. The stone the builder rejected has become the cornerstone; washing hands is the most popular theory in science and has even become law. All personnel in hospitals and clinics who provide direct or indirect care must wash their hands before touching a patient; it is a universal law.

Your lovely companion believed there is no universal essence in each man, but the latest discovery in biology suggests the opposite. The information-bearing property inside our bodies is a strong argument against his philosophy. Indeed, there is Information in all living organisms that encodes life on Earth; this set of information gives humans a specific nature. We have a personality that is manifested as a particular frequency in the seminal mind. Personhood frequency makes us who we are and distinguishes us from animals and objects. Like animals, we are subjects living within a material object, but humans have that frequency of personhood[6] to separate them from the animal kingdom. When that frequency of personhood does not resonate with its source (God or pure consciousness), we call it ego. Sigmund Freud mainly worked on this topic, and you never ceased quoting him in your masterpiece, "The Second Sex." Freud sees the ego as the portion of the psyche that emerges to confront reality. In my philosophy, the ego is the part of the non-flesh entity that vibrates away from its source.

---

[6] To have a thorough understanding of the frequency of personhood, check our paper on ssrn.com, the Elsevier repository for scientific and philosophical research; the article is free for download. Zanou, A. (2021) "Could Humanoid Robots Become Conscious?" Social Science Research Network [Elsevier]

The ego is one particular state of the frequency of personhood in the same way ice is one state of liquid water. When the frequency of personhood is severed from the source (God or pure consciousness), we refer to it as the ego. Whenever the frequency of personhood vibrates opposite to its source, I call it ego. So, the ego is not something special but one particular state of the individual's mind. As we know today, a person is a particular state of consciousness that is characterized by self-awareness, power, force, volition (Desire and Reason), judgment, purpose, beliefs, and the quest for knowledge; the list is not exhaustive.

My Dear Simone, rejecting God didn't help you advance your feminist arguments. There is a universal essence behind this material world. Like a tree and its root, existence, and life share the same analogy. The manifestation of the root generates the tree. While the root lies underground, unseen to the human eyes, the tree is displayed outside and can be apprehended by our senses. So be it of existence and life. Existence occurs in the material world and can be divided into material and living existence. Life resides in the immaterial realm and is still a mystery to us, and we don't know much about it. However, some of its characteristics fall broadly within our ken. We know the author of life also has a frequency of personhood. He is also a person possessing the following attributes: omnipresence, omniscience, omnipotence, and creativity.

The same life that is manifested in men is also expressed through women, but changes occur during the expression. Today, we know that when the heart pumps blood to the brain, consciousness is displayed on the screen of the mind as Will and Representation. In the Will, we have

Desire governed by Reason. In the Representation, we have Memory and Perception.

The difference between man and woman lies in the manifestation of the Will and the Representation. While women have a beautiful and harmonious Representation, men, on the contrary, see chaos and darkness. I disagreed when Pythagoras said, "There is a good principle that created order, light, and man and a bad principle that created chaos, darkness, and woman." How could the Greek thinker be right? Women don't make war. They don't go gallivanting around the city. Who rapes women? War and rape are not order and light. Women promote harmony; they give birth and care, while men kill and destroy. How wrong could Pythagoras be? To say that the Greek scholar is correct means that the carceral population is mostly female, but the reality shows the opposite. Worldwide, there are more men in jail than women; it is a fact. I thank Descartes for opening our eyes and delivering the world from the domination of the Greek schools of philosophy. Pythagoras was wrong, dear ma'am; as I have said already, beware of the Greeks. Descartes warns us.

Besides the botched and ugly Representation men have, their Desire is also awful. Women long for affection and attention. Men crave sex, money, and power, and they spend their existence warring for these three things. The tragedy of our planet is written with these three elements, which dominate men's Desire. Often men misapprehend love for lust, value for money, and beliefs for power. They misunderstand the actual definition of these three elements and bring disaster and calamity to our world. Power lures men to superiority, control, and domination, sex to depravity and debauchery, and money to pillaging and plundering.

To me, there is a good principle that creates order, light, and woman and a bad principle that produces chaos, darkness, and men. In my philosophy, women stand on the bright side of the force while men wallow in the dark side, but science apprehends the situation differently. According to science, the original light, which is pure consciousness from the immaterial realm, undergoes degeneration as the system moves from a ground state to an excited state. The breaking symmetry of the system causes an explosion or inflation that begets the material world. Chaos emerges and moves out of the immaterial realm alongside Information and Order. The concatenation of Information, Order, and chaos gives birth to material objects in which life is manifested as male and female.

There is only one unique principle that bifurcates man and woman. Sadly, men stand on the dark side of the force while women portray its bright side. Notice that men don't get pregnant; women do. Women are the guardians of life, the reproductive principle perpetuating the human species. Undoubtedly, men are the active branch of the force, and they produce while women reproduce, making women the passive branch. That's why women have a womb.

Reproduction is not a curse as you thought it to be; it is a gift only if things work according to the agenda of life. I agree and stand by your side when you describe women's pregnancy as a tedious job. Not only the task of carrying a pregnancy is mind-numbing, but it is also the deadliest of all mammals' accouchements. For that cause, pregnancy cannot be free; your compatriot actress and author Nadine de Rothschild shared the same vision. She had always advocated for paid domestic labor. Our daughters must not get pregnant with bums and vagabonds. We must teach them to identify and steer clear of boys and immature males. They must be able to distinguish dating from a marital relationship and understand the responsibility that underlines the latter. Men move by sexual impulses and often confound lust with love. A man is not a woman, and our daughters must know how men think. As I have said earlier, both men and women don't have the same Representation of the world, and their volitions differ. Girls and Women have a natural propensity for settling and building a home. Boys and men prefer gallivanting around the city. They tend to settle when their ambitions for sex, money, and power are appeased. To navigate correctly and safely through this life, our daughters need to understand existence and how it unfolds. Failure to grasp the meanders of existence will result in much trouble. That's why many women suffer. They suffer not because men are cruel but because our girls are ignorant of these facts. Here is what I want them to know:

First, our daughters need to distinguish life from existence. Second, they must differentiate between man and woman, and third, they must watch for the demarcation line separating dating from marital relationships. Here is the gospel I am preaching. Like Paul, I am the apostle of the youth, specially appointed for our daughters to break away from the chains and get out of men's grip. Parents are crushed and misinformed; our professionals have no cognizance because they have made an error in incorporating the mind into the body. The mind is not a part of the body; the brain is. Humans are not solely flesh, and both men and women are different.

First Distinction: Life and Existence

Life is still a mystery, but one of our goals is to demystify it. Thus, the first challenge is to define it; even scientists continue to struggle with its definition. Scientists' current definition is flawed because life is more than a self-sustaining chemical system; it is not a mere chemical reaction. The reason why scientists think life is a simple chemical reaction is because of materialism. Scientific materialism pushes its agenda and maintains that life is about synthetic organic chemistry. If it is, why do we die? Why do living organisms die? If the vital energy comes from the mitochondria, why do these organelles need functional Information to operate? Scientists often forget there is DNA in the mitochondria, meaning these organelles cannot function without practical Information.

Life emanates from the immaterial realm and is manifested in the material world, which can be apprehended scientifically; the manifestation of life is graspable. Existence always arches over birth and death. While the study of life itself is difficult because of its immaterial aspect, its manifestation, on the contrary, is within our ken. Your fellow citizen Frederic Saldmann said human existence must span over 120 years, and any death before that is premature. If I consider his scale and know that no human falls from the sky, I can distinguish two sessions in the development of the individual. These two sessions are labeled training and solo sessions.

The training session starts from birth until the individual proclaims her independence and leaves the parental house.

The baby always sojourns in a woman's womb and is born after forty weeks. All newborns have at least one caregiver. Human society is so organized that no baby is left alone at birth. Someone will always be there. By the time the infant acquires awareness and self-awareness, she will find herself with someone. While some babies are lucky to have two caregivers, some don't have the same opportunity. But what two parents can do, one can also perform.

Whether two parents or not, the adult that welcomes the baby must stand as a caregiver; she must train and educate the girl for a definite period. As Rousseau had said in the first book of "Emile, ou de l'Education," "our first tutor is our nanny." The caregiver must not raise the child to keep her because many parents eventually do that; many see a child as property and have difficulty dissolving the parental bond to let the kid go once she becomes an adult. Even after leaving the parental house, parents are still in control behind the scene. Therefore, they fail to raise the kid to become independent. We love our children too much that we forget what parenthood is truly about: educating kids. In chapter 9 of the book's second volume, you describe the situation very well.; too many people are unaware that parental bonds must be dissolved at twenty-one; they condemn their children to eternal childhood. Some parents even go to war against their in-laws, proving the child is not truly independent. As you nicely write it:

"Normally, the grandmother overcomes her hostility; sometimes she obstinately sees the newborn as her son's alone, and she loves it tyrannically; but generally, the young mother and her own mother claim it for their own; the jealous grandmother cultivates an ambiguous affection for the baby, where hostility hides in the guise of concern."

The grandmother must have a life on her own; she had one before conceiving and must still have one after the kid grows up and leaves the house. When I often speak of this phenomenon, people see me as a lunatic, but you have just nailed it. I don't fabricate it; humans don't understand existence and why they have kids. The lives of parents must be dissociated from their children's lives once they leave the house; too many people don't understand that, and the phenomenon impedes the development of the kids because too many children fail to deploy their programs. While human society is changing, existence does not change; it remains challenging. And the child is called to bring her modest contribution to the community later when she becomes an adult; parents must bear that in mind. Society requires something from the kid as an adult; thus, parents must train and educate her according to the community's demands. There is always something the community asks from every kid; our daughters need to be aware of such reality; it is called duty[7].

Beyond the responsibilities of the individual and the rights the community offers in return, the individual has the basic duties, which include the duty to respect the neighbors, pay taxes, be drafted, and defend the territory when it is invaded. The individual could serve as a government

---

[7] We explain the responsibilities, rights and duties of the individual within a modern society in our dissertation "The Social Fabric;" It is an addendum to the social contract theory discussed by the European thinkers during the Enlightenment Era. The essay is available on Amazon KDP.

member to manage the community with her expertise. Duties are obligations the individual owes the community; they are mandatory, and their violation could terminate her membership. In the olden days, people who failed in their duties toward the community were usually ostracized. Parents must bring up the child to have full cognizance of her duties in this modern society; failure to do so often brings dire consequences that could lead to anarchy and revolt, as we notice today.

The solo session is where the girl flies away for her solo life. Here is where most trouble befalls our daughters. The majority of our girls don't know that adult life is challenging, and many forget they have a womb. Nature designed them as a receptacle to receive whatever boys shoot at them. As we know, no one continually fills a jar without expecting the water to overflow. One day, the water level will come to the brim and spill out. A girl who continually beds with a man must be prepared that things will go wrong one day or right if the boy is financially prepared. Sex is sweet, but our daughters need to know that they bear more consequences than boys. Both meet to partake in the pleasure, but only girls carry the burden of pregnancy. Yes, pregnancy is a problem when one is not ready, and it becomes a burden when the boy does not want to hear anything about it. Boys don't want to hear anything about pregnancy, but men are always prepared for it. For that cause, our daughters need to know the difference between a man and a boy.

A boy is a lad who does not know where he is going. He comes to seek pleasure and has no resources to handle any consequences that could ensue. A man is a pilot who has a roadmap; he understands modern society and knows woman's constitution. He comes to give pleasure because he knows female sexuality is complex, and by giving, he allows both partners to reach satisfaction. A man always has some resources available because he knows nothing is really free in human society. One must pay something to receive anything. A man also bears in mind that coitus always has two consequences.

In addition to the first consequence, pleasure, pregnancy always lurks in the dark, a latent outcome. And women are designated to carry the burden. If our daughters ignore this fact, nobody can blame boys. Everyone is called to protect his assets, and it is the responsibility of our daughters to know. Since the Garden of Eden, our ancestors chose the pathway of knowledge; therefore, we must be good at it.

Three fundamental elements characterize the solo session. First, it is challenging; second, it is about timing; and finally, it is about investment. Women agonize because they have no cognizance of such things. Men also suffer, but since they live by transcendence, as you said, they cope with their suffering better. Women thrive in immanence; therefore, they must carefully pay attention to their existence. They need to be aware of their status to take advantage of this life. As I said earlier, when two individuals, a man and a woman, meet in sexual interactions, the woman bears two consequences while the man gets away with pleasure only. A man does not carry a pregnancy; a woman does. Today, modern society has devised a plan to make boys pay for the violation as alimony, but girls always bear the consequence in their flesh. It is unfair when two individuals share an intense moment of joy, and one has to carry the outcome in her flesh. Is God biased? No!

God himself is not divided, but his manifestation is differential. Hence, both men and women need each other to carry on life's agenda. The machinery of life requires both man and woman as complementary entities. Humans cause the manifestation of God to weigh upon us because of their ignorance; they have created doctrines out of the expression of God to harm each other. God always sees man and woman together, living in harmony in an obligatory symbiotic relationship. He perceives them as complementing and completing each other.

The differentiation process provides different timing for both men and women. Both individuals are not on the same clock, and women must be aware of it. In the olden days, the investment section also is different for boys and girls, but today, this gap is filled up. Parents are the first investors in the life of the kids, and the primary investment occurs in a particular place called school. Since adulthood is exclusively challenging, modern society requests we train children to meet the challenges ahead; hence, we provide instructions to our kids.

In the late years of the age of assimilation, which runs from birth to seven years, parents everywhere in modern society grab the hands of the kid and bring her to a facility. They sit down with the headmaster of the place and tell him indirectly to train the kid so that she may learn how to make money and seduce an excellent partner in the future. That's what life is about: making money and attracting a partner. People who understand it are good citizens, assisting the community in reaching its full potential; those who fail to grasp the concept have become what Wattles Wallace called "a deadweight upon society."

Existence is a lifelong investment process, and once the individual stops learning, she starts dying. We must keep investing in ourselves continually; we are here to learn and grow. For that cause, we separate the individual's existence into two separate portions: training session and solo session.

The first session unfolds under the supervision of our parents or caregivers and runs from birth to twenty-one years of age. It is divided into three distinct periods: the age of assimilation, the age of reason, and the age of consciousness.

As I said earlier, the age of assimilation spreads from birth to seven years old. Self-awareness and personhood are two frequencies of the seminal mind that get activated in this particular period of the infant's development. We must not confound self-awareness frequency with self-awareness operation, which occurs later in the age of consciousness. Today, science still doesn't know when this particular awakening occurs in the child's body systems. However, we know that the phenomenon happens during the age of assimilation, which spreads from birth to seven years old, and most schooling starts during the same period. Almost all children gain self-awareness before reaching seven years old; those who fail might probably have congenital malformation.

The age of reason runs from seven to fourteen years old. This period could also be called the age of menarche for girls because most girls worldwide experience their first menstruation. This period is characterized by profound physical changes in the girl's body. The physical details are well-known to scientists, but inside turmoil still eludes researchers. As a human being is a man and woman inside, the woman begins to have ascendancy over the man, and the female starts expressing herself as a girl. The opposite happens in the male body: the man rises and dominates the woman. I will open up broadly on this phenomenon later.

The struggle between the man and woman inside the body system is not understood by science, and psychologists often apprehend the phenomenon badly. They advise parents based on the assumption that humans are solely flesh. As a result, we have chaotic adolescence, especially in the West and the US. Instead of looking inward to find a solution, modern psychology recommends teenagers look outside. Some run after sex to handle the trouble. Instead of providing a solution, many pour gasoline on the fire and worsen the situation. Some girls become pregnant, and many girls who hurry their defloration later regret it. The mind was not ready for sexuality.

Girls receive the act during intimacy. The womb is a receptacle, and the vagina often comes with a seal, and how we remove it matters. Welcoming a man inside her is always a delicate business for young girls, and our daughters must be prepared for it. The anxiety that overwhelms the body is proof the individual is not ready. Humans are sexual beings; therefore, sex must come naturally. Young people hiding to copulate is evidence sexuality is not the business of adolescents. The study shows that the first experience has a tremendous impact on the sexuality of women in the future, while men are indifferent. You provided a long list of defloration cases and how they occurred in chapter 8 of the book's second volume. The first time is always a traumatic event for girls when the experience does not go well; sex must be done in confidence and with total relaxation. And often, men don't regret their first experience, but most women do. It is so because many girls lack the necessary information about the act. Most girls didn't know what they were doing, trusting the boy, who was also a novice most of the time. We have to admit modern society does not provide sexual education to the youth, and many folks live in the dark. Very few are aware sexuality is an adult business; some see it as a ticket to becoming an adult, hence the urgent need to get rid of their virginity.

Adolescence is a particular period that slips through the fingers of youngsters. Parents have little information, and many assist their children helplessly. Science has already made the error of incorporating the mind into the body; the mind is not a part of the body; the brain is. Nobody quite understands what is happening in teenagers' minds, and because parents cannot grasp whatever their children are going through, some set up drastic measures in the house. Others allow their children to have sex since it is the only thing that best relaxes the body.

Nonage is the most turbulent period in the individual's life that is characterized by an unceasing battle in mind. The immaterial components are in turmoil, and hormones flush the body systems without control; this situation causes depression in adolescence. All teenagers experience generalized malaise caused by these strange activities between the spirit, soul, and mind. As we define him, a human being is a spiritual being who lives in a body, has a soul, and operates with a mind. The spirit is an electromagnetic field hovering over the heart; the soul is the activity over the blood, and the mind is the field hovering over the brain. The three electromagnetic fields come together and generate the immaterial components; the three organs involved (heart, blood, and brain) have intense activities during the age of reason and will continue throughout the age of consciousness.

The last period is the age of consciousness, and it spreads from fourteen to twenty-one years of age. I call it the age of consciousness because it is the period that transitions between childhood and adulthood, where the individual secedes from his parents to deploy his God given program. Since some people identify consciousness to God, the age of consciousness refers to the moment the individual gets ready to serve. It's here the self-awareness operation occurs. Ancient cultures recommended the individual do the self-awareness operation before entering adulthood. In the olden days, society focused on boys and initiated them before entering the solo session. The Buddhists called this operation "Enlightenment." Muslims labeled it "Jihad," while Christians know it as "Born Again," and the Greeks said, "Know Thyself."

During the self-awareness operation, the individual is called to know who she is, what she wants, and where she is going. Life's journey is more accessible and enjoyable when the individual knows herself, what she wants, and her destination. A ship at sea will get lost if the captain does not know which direction to steer; he can only set his course correctly if he has the destination harbor in mind. Those who lack such information about themselves are more likely to mess up and struggle through the journey. If the individual knows where she is going, she can spot a potential partner walking the same pathway.

In this modern society, the best age to get the self-awareness operation done is seventeen or eighteen because significant errors occur at these ages; usually, this moment corresponds to the period where the individual either graduates from High school or quits. Her decision in the aftermath is critical; unfortunately, many mess up at this step of their lives. Most individuals who struggle and suffer in adulthood make their mistakes during this period of their existence. One of the fundamental errors that often destroy young girls forever is pregnancy. Getting pregnant is an unexpected event that mars the young girl's existence, and girls often don't recover from this mistake. Very few girls succeed in straightening things up and coming back on track.

The age of consciousness is not designed for sexuality, although the intense urge for intimacy. Notice that most achievers, scientists, and great thinkers lay hands on their talents before engaging in sexuality. Science does not fully understand how this phenomenon unfolds, but the observation shows that most achievers know about their gifts and are well-focused before engaging in sexuality. We know gene expressions code for proteins that build the body. Thus, during gene expressions, organs designated to serve the purpose of our dominant Information have more attention than others. Early sex compromises the process as pleasure storms the body systems and chaos settles. The entire phenomenon is not well understood yet.

Howbeit, the inward battle between the immaterial components increases chaos in the body, causing the dominant Information we carry in our DNA to float. Our existence unfolds according to the Information in our chromosomes.

Some special codons in our genetic material are designed to help individuals achieve extraordinary things; we live to solve problems. That's what adulthood is about: solving problems and becoming happy. We live in a community, and society requires making some contributions. Those who lay hands on their gifts solve significant challenges in our society. Nowadays, things have changed tremendously, and most talents are not solving problems but entertaining us. Today, our celebrities sing and perform in theaters to amuse us after a hectic workday. In the olden days, engineers, miracle workers, physicians, magicians, preachers, healers, and recently, scientists were people who occupied the spotlight. They dedicated their talents to solving significant issues in our communities. The world has progressed because of these achievers.

Talents come up to the surface during the age of consciousness for the majority of the case. Sometimes, these special codons get activated during the age of assimilation, as it had been for Friedrich Gauss, Michael Jackson, and Wolfgang Amadeus Mozart. The gifts sprang up on their own for these kids, and the individual trained himself to polish them and bring them to fruition. As I have said earlier, science is late understanding and explaining the phenomenon. However, we know that particular organs involved in manifesting talents have special attention during protein synthesis in the body. For instance, singers would have their vocal cords strengthened and built up in specific ways. Genes expression will favor building up the leg of dancers and athlete sprinters, while thinkers will have their neurons in the brain wired up in particular ways. These things don't occur randomly; they follow specific programs.

The three periods of assimilation, reason, and consciousness constitute the training session and must end at twenty-one years of age. Children are called to proclaim their independence and secede from the parental house at twenty-one to build their own nest. For that cause, parents must provide adequate training for the kid so that she can fly alone after leaving the parental house. Sadly, many girls seem to struggle after leaving the house, and it is so because the equation has new parameters. Modern society has new inputs that make the equation of life challenging to solve, but the child must fly solo no matter what.

The authority of parents stops at twenty-one, and the kid's responsibility begins whenever she is ready. While young girls must be aware of the restriction time imposes on their existence because of pregnancy, boys, on the other hand, must focus on investment. At an early age, the young girl must decide whether she wants kids or not. This particular decision must be made during the self-awareness operation, which we know occurs during the age of consciousness.

A young girl who wants children cannot live haphazardly because her time is ticking unless she plans to adopt a kid. Whether we accept it or not, a womb remains the asset of a girl who wants to marry and build a family. For that cause, she cannot waste her time with boys. We live in a free society, and people can live the way they want it. However, we must be aware that how we live impacts society. Man and woman are designed differently, and we cannot ignore it. Failure to take heed of human biology is one of the causes of women's struggle. A girl who does not want a kid has already escaped the grip of time and is free to enjoy life as she pleases.

Humans struggle because they lack knowledge. It's not that existence is troublesome because it unfolds following a well-defined pattern. Most of our trouble emanates from the wrong philosophy and ideology we have developed over time. Despite the blatant evidence, we still believe life has no meaning and purpose. How is that possible? First of all, we need to grasp these two words: meaning and purpose. Now that we can differentiate between life and existence, we must define meaning and purpose to determine if life and existence unfold according to their definitions. People often use meaning and purpose interchangeably; they do the same thing with life and existence. Meanwhile, they are not the same, although they share many similarities.

Purpose accomplishes while meaning intends. Purpose connotes a goal, and meaning is the action we deploy to reach the goal. Thus, when we mean the purpose of life, we search for whatever life is accomplishing, while the meaning of life will look for how life unfolds to reach that goal.

That said, we can boldly state that the purpose of life is multiplication and growth. Every living organism in this material world tends to grow and multiply. All scientists agree that life starts with a single cell that develops and reproduces to give diversity to the species we have in the world. If a single cell could become such a diverse species, it is without any doubt that the goal of life is to grow and multiply.

Since life appears on Earth, it has continually struggled to multiply and grow. And to do this, life uses a technique that brings two complementary entities together to copulate. Today, we know that technique as love; therefore, life's meaning is love. Through the mating of living organisms, life reaches its goal. The German philosopher Arthur Schopenhauer believes life tricks and inveigles living beings to copulate and reproduce[8].

The meaning of life is love, and through love, life gets its purpose. Right now, the will-to-life is pushing humans to spread throughout the universe. Life does not want to be confined on Earth alone; it intends to scatter through the galaxy. And sooner or later, humans will move out to explore the solar system and other galaxies.

The Vikings killed and murdered people during their raids; Francisco Pizzaro worked hard to wipe out the Inca people, and Adolf Hitler labored to exterminate the Jews. Hutu and Tutsi in Rwanda butchered each other, yet life managed to survive, and today, we are seven billion souls roaming the planet. Life always has its way of counteracting its annihilation; it has all the necessary resources to support existence in this material universe.

While the purpose of life is multiplication and growth and is independent of the individual's agenda, existence, on the contrary, is contingent on the individual's volition. The purpose and meaning of existence are whatever we make our lives to be. Existence is one particular frequency of life; it is up to the individual to handle that frequency as she pleases. Although a well-defined program is written in our DNA,

---

[8] Schopenhauer exposes in chapter 44: The Metaphysics of the love of the sexes, how two opposite sexes manage to perpetuate the human species. Schopenhauer, A. (2012) "The World as Will and Idea," Translated by R. Haldane and J. Kemp; Vol III. Sixth Edition, Trubner & Co. London

the individual has the final say over his destiny. Nowadays, a woman can decide what she wants to make of her life. They were wombs, a reproductive machine to supply warriors for the city and the king in the olden days, but today, things are different. That's why young girls must understand these aspects of human existence to make genuine life decisions.

Women continue to suffer because they don't have cognizance of these things. During the self-awareness operation, the boys have one fundamental choice to make, and the girls two. Boys and girls must decide in which pool they want their lives to unfold because existence on Earth unwinds in two different pools: celibacy and partnership. If the individual is not in the first pool, she is necessary for the second one. The youth must refrain from fooling themselves. There is no other alternative; it is one pool or the other.

The pool of celibacy comprises clergymen, monks, nuns, and spiritual individuals who have devoted their lives to serving the purpose of life. They separated themselves from the crowd and set themselves apart to study and understand life to serve its purpose well. For that cause, they are guides for those who live in a partnership. They set their lives apart to assist and help people who choose to live in alliance for a better society. They intercede, pray, and advise married couples and their children because they have devoted their existence to understanding the manifestation of life on Earth, and they grasp it better.

If the individual is not in the pool of celibacy, she is necessarily in the partnership pool. Here, individuals team up to make existence comfortable and fulfill the purpose of life. They come together to build the unit of production known as a family. In the erstwhile society, a family is composed of a male and several females for reproduction purposes. Nowadays, the definition is broad and diverse, and not all families can reproduce.

Reproduction is one particular aspect of the existence of the young girl. For that cause, she is called to make an additional choice during the self-awareness operation. Thus, young girls must also choose between preservation or reproduction. It is so because females have a ticking clock that young girls must not ignore. Girls who choose to preserve their bodies have more freedom because they can live haphazardly. Those who choose reproduction cannot and must be aware that their womb is an asset.

A womb has no value for a girl who chooses preservation. In this case, pregnancy for her is a burden. As you put it nicely, pregnancy is a gift and a curse. It is a gift for young girls who opt for reproduction and a curse for those who don't want to reproduce. We are free to say no to life; Arthur Schopenhauer calls us to rebel, giving us an example. He lived what he preached, and I could tell you did the same.

Once young girls understand these choices and set themselves up, existence becomes easy. Women struggle because many don't make any choice; they let life or someone decide for them. Nowadays, nobody can choose for young girls, and everything is in their own hands. Boys make one fundamental choice, and girls make two.

Girls who choose partnership and reproduction must refrain from wasting time with boys. Life is a choice; it is nowadays. People suffer because they are indecisive. Some individuals are still allowing society or their parents to determine for them. Parents can influence our choices, but they cannot decide for us because they will not live existence in our stead. One of the purposes of our existence is happiness; we live to be satisfied; thus, we must be the main actors in our lives.

As the word pops up, let's delve into it. Happiness is what everybody is seeking, although many live in denial. Nobody decides to marry and get into the street to grab the first individual she spots; it does not work that way. When people shop for their groceries, they scrutinize their items for defects, comparing the prices before deciding. Why do they do that? They are looking for happiness. All economists agree that the consumer is seeking satisfaction; it always does. All humans look for happiness, and people who say the opposite are fooling themselves because their lifestyles testify for them. They wear nice clothes and drive fancy cars; why? The purpose of a car is to pick the individual from one point to another; any jalopy can do that.

Today, women may consider men lucky because nature does not impose on them as it does on women. In the olden days, our mothers and sisters didn't see someone who continually put his life at risk as fortunate. More men die in battles than women could die at home if no aggressors invaded the village to rape and kill. Humanity has evolved so that we amend our society. For that cause, women need to understand life, existence, and modern society. Failure to comprehend this phenomenon is the cause of pandemonium in our communities. The youth must be willing to learn. Young girls must understand; otherwise, they will continue blaming a system that eventually is changing. Women need a role to play; they are in the first line in this battle to amend our society because they bear children and spend more time with them than anyone else. Children are closer to their mothers than their fathers, no matter what we say. It is natural; biology is at play here instead of ideology. Technically, children belong to their mothers, and this statement is also true in the animal kingdom, with only a few exceptions. They sojourn in their womb for forty weeks, and both have developed a strong connection. The world will eventually change if women reconsider the situation. More befall their hands than they may think. Life is a childhood preparation, and children copy their parents' behavior. Often, a woman who becomes a mother at seventeen is more likely to have her girl pregnant at a young age. These patterns are common in our society; we don't notice them because we are too busy in a world that never ceases to be noisy.

It is easy to blame someone for the trouble in our lives; everywhere else, that is what everybody does. Therefore, we must educate our children differently. A new generation with a novel mindset could change the situation; we need a new mentality. Women need to seize the opportunity to implement the necessary change our society needs. Modern society offers many favorable options, and women must stop perceiving themselves as victims. In the past, they were victims, but today, more power is at their disposal.

Understanding the whole picture in this modern society depends on our daughter's ability to distinguish life from existence and grasp the constitution of man and woman. There is one point I agree with in your entire philosophy and throughout your book that I could never disagree with is that we must exist first. Your beloved companion, Jean-Paul Sartre, wisely put it: existentialism is humanism. The world is in trouble because we don't take the time to be human beings first. We want to be Ukrainians, Russians, or members of NATO; we want to be Black or White first. Our ultimate desire is to be something before we exist. We want to be American, French, British, Germans, Chinese, Japanese, Canadians, or Nigerians before anything else. We toil to be Republicans, Democrats, Liberals, or Conservatives first. What if we exist first? Notice how ideologies drain humans nowadays; it was not different in your era. Through nationalist propaganda, Adolf Hitler drove several million souls to slaughter.

We must be human beings first. Our struggle on this planet is unnecessary; we suffer because we don't know how to live. Many look in the mirror and cannot accept what they see; hence, they strive to love themselves. Our daughters cannot like themselves without acknowledging themselves first. They need self-esteem, and they can never get it unless they exist first. The more the individual makes errors, the less likely she will like herself.

The youth need to understand Sartre's plea on existentialism. We must exist first, as human beings, before we can do or be anything else; it is what I call be-to-think. As humans, we have an essence. We are spiritual beings encased in physical bodies, and the concatenation of the immaterial components and the physical body is called a human being. Before pretending to be scientists, Buddhists, Christians, Muslims, or philosophers, we must be human beings first; the journey on Earth is an adventure for human beings.

There is trouble in our world because people usually think to be. Humans have chosen the model think-to-be as their reality, and the world has a problem. The human brain is a filter and cannot account for the totality of the manifestation of life. Our vision limits us; science says humans can only see less than one percent of the electromagnetic spectrum, represented by the visible band. The visible spectrum is the tiny portion of the electromagnetic spectrum the human eyes can detect; this means whatever is happening around us is only limited to a small band, and we call it reality. As long as humans are concerned, the real is what they can see; how ludicrous is that! The manifestation of life goes beyond our visions. We should humble ourselves if we consider how vast the electromagnetic spectrum is, yet perceived only through the narrow visible band. The observation shows that animals behave conspicuously before an earthquake. How do they know? Are there phenomena humans cannot perceive? Scientists killed Ignaz Semmelweis when he invoked the existence of a tiny world unseen to humans. His germs theory brought him into trouble; his colleagues rejected his idea because society lacked the necessary tools to observe microscopic creatures in those days. Germs were later accepted when Louis Pastor proved them through his vaccine experiments, and the scientific community finally admitted a world smaller than ours could exist. These physicians who killed Semmelweis believed they knew it all, but they were wrong.

I stand with Sartre in this sense that we must exist as human beings first because we are not on a spiritual journey, although we are spiritual beings. Most people think we are on a spiritual journey, but we are not. The non-flesh entity cannot operate without a body; as he is encased in a physical body, we call the combination a human being. Therefore, we are on a human journey, and for that cause, we need to be humans before starting the journey; the spirit must incarnate first. Any spirit that fails to pick up the body after accouchement cannot operate in the terrestrial environment. The physical body is the passport to function on Earth; he who loses his passport will be kicked out; we call it death.

I cannot entirely agree with Sartre that we have total control of our lives; we don't, but a good portion of our existence falls into our hands. We are the pilots of our existence on Earth to a certain degree; I also believe in the essentialism of Plato[9]. I perceive human existence at the crossroads between essentialism and existentialism. Throughout the course of the individual's life, some battles can fall upon her, which she cannot decline. One can be a man of peace and be dragged into a war; he can stand for love and be compelled to hate. One can be just and forced to sit with the unjust, but on balance, the individual is still the master of his ship amid chaos.

The non-flesh entity operates his vessel but must be aware of many other parameters that escape human understanding. While existence follows definite patterns, life does not. Too many unknown parameters intervene in

---

[9] Plato exposed an aspect of his essentialist philosophy in his dialogue "Cratylus," in sections 384-389, where the interlocutors discussed the nature of reality. Socrates argued that the truth spreads beyond words and names we give to things; the truth resides in a place where things have permanent and unchanging nature. In the Parmenides, Plato delved into the theory of Forms or Ideas and expanded it.

our existence to make it a puzzle. Here is a story to illustrate my point.

The Story of Sergeant Kamoki can make you question existentialist philosophy; we are not in complete control of our existence, are we? I know you have become an atheist like your companion, but life is not as simple as the existentialist philosophers pretend it to be. I would prefer to see you agnostic than an atheist because you were reared Catholic; it seems like the setbacks of the Church had strengthened your conviction, but you made the wrong choice. Reincarnation is one great reason the individual has no total control of his life. When previous life memories influence our current living, we must be careful to admit we are in total control of our existence. The presence of functional Information in our chromosomes is also a great argument to deploy against existentialism. The story goes this way:

While on duty one sunny afternoon, two republican guards approached the sergeant to instruct him about the upcoming coup against the president-dictator. The young sergeant didn't say no; he didn't say yes either. His comrades, afraid that he might blow the whistle, slit his throat in his indecisiveness.

The sergeant was murdered before his shift ended at the presidential palace. How can you explain that? What did Sergeant Kamoki do wrong? He neither agreed nor disagreed. His colleagues killed him because he could not decide like a man, and he died from his indecisiveness.

Did the sergeant choose to die? Sartre believed humans have the power to choose, and I agree with him, but sometimes, events are imposed on us, and we can do nothing about them. Women never choose to have a womb; it was imposed on them because nobody ever asked their opinion. Sergeant Kamoki didn't determine anything either. While some may move through this existence without scratches, some will have their lives bombarded by misfortune. As a Christian philosopher, I believe all events, whether good or bad, work together for good if we yield to the force. But in the tale above, things didn't work well for Sergeant Kamoki unless we justified death as a good thing. Nobody wants to die, at least not that way.

While we don't necessarily control what befalls us, we have the power to manage what happens to us; that's the philosophy of the stoics, but in our story, Sergeant Kamoki didn't have the chance to handle the situation. He was caught off guard. What would Sartre say about Sergeant Kamoki's tragic story?

It is undeniable that our lives do not unreel solely following existentialist patterns. Some portions of our existence unfold with the essentialism components. We don't cause tsunamis or earthquakes; nobody calls upon floods or tornadoes. The Jews never called upon them the Nazis and the Aztec people didn't attract Hernan Cortez. African people never desired to be enslaved; it came upon them. I have seen hailstorms destroy people's brand-new cars and homes. Some are born with disabilities; others grow healthy, become ill, and die too soon. Do people choose any of these things? Some illnesses are traceable to the genetic material; do we determine which genes to inherit? People don't choose their parents, do they?

People often say we don't choose our families; we are born to discover that we live in a certain place. Everyone would desire to be born in a palace, at least poor people, because they have experienced poverty already; they know what it is to live in scarcity. Life is not pleasant when you are a pauper. No matter how poor people comfort themselves and their children, poverty is not a desirable condition. They may scream that money does not bring happiness, but everybody knows it is better to cry in a Lamborghini than to ride a bicycle. With my current knowledge of human society, I would pick Oprah Winfrey as a mother and Bill Gates as a father if I had to choose my parents. Perhaps I saw them but decided to land in Togo instead. At Ecole Naval, I discovered one of my assignments was to become the president of Togo; I abandoned that pathway because I was not well-prepared. Life is a childhood preparation, and my parents have no clue about it, so this program slips through my fingers.

A nascent theory suggests humans might have been choosing their families; I do personally believe in this latter hypothesis. The probability is high that people decide where they want to be born; my story above is one piece of evidence, although it is a subjective experience. I got the necessary resources to perform the job; the Information is locked up in my chromosomes, but my parents were blind to giving direction to my talent. The story reports that Lady Gaga's mother spotted her child's ability and offered her a piano so that she could develop her gift. Parents who are awake and understand their role play it well. Mark Zuckerberg's father was said to be behind his child's success; he noticed the activated gift and provided a vent for developing the child's talent.

Another example is Papa Williams. The anecdote reports that he saw Virginia Ruzici playing tennis on TV and decided his daughters would be professional tennis players. He coached his daughters to meet that goal. While some are aware of their child-rearing role as parents and take it seriously, others are lousy and negligent.

One must be aware that the fundamental program we carry flashes on the screen of our mind when we are about to doze off; when our alertness and attention weaken, the most dominant programs of our systems come up and display in front of us. One must understand that God is love, and love gives, forgives, and serves. If the individual's program deals with killing, mass shootings, racism, sexism, xenophobia, and violence of all kinds, his original program might have been corrupted. God is good all the time, and he is pure consciousness, a concatenation of Information and Order.

Similar to viruses that hijack the cell's machinery to produce more viruses, the rebellion code can take over some people's Information systems. In that case, it is better for the individual to seek the assistance of an expert or a psychologist. Rihanna's primary Information is to entertain people. Lady Gaga's most dominant program is to compose and sing songs. Serena Williams plays tennis, and Rosalind Franklin has a wit for photographing complex structures. As an individual, if your Information is not serving humanity, it probably does not come from the source of life. The special codon that gives humans extraordinary abilities must proceed from pure consciousness, and we know it must stand for service, forgiveness, and giving.

This tempting hypothesis[10] is based on the fact that humans are medium consciousness serving as the intermediate between God and the rest of the creation. The presence of the DNA molecules inside our bodies seems to corroborate this hypothesis. The manifestation of pure consciousness is divided into medium and lower consciousness. Humans, as mediators, toil to reconcile the creation with God. Thus, the spirit incarnates on Earth for a specific purpose, and children choose their parents.

The theory might sound absurd, but there is one particular case scientists have investigated that pulls things together. A young boy from Louisiana was traumatized by previous life memories. The psychiatrist Jim Tucker studied the case and published an article following his investigation titled "The Case of James Leininger: An American Case of the Reincarnation Type."

In his own words, the boy stated that he chose his parents. There was a television interview on the case, but it never aired, probably because of skepticism. What if we choose our parents? We can be born to solve some particular problem in our community; Newton did it, and so did Einstein. Some spiritual gurus believe some individuals incarnate to bring

---

[10] This hypothesis goes along with Sartre's vision of existence: we are free to decide what we want to be because we are already equipped and have full Will to carry out our agenda. Sartre exposed his view on human existence in the public lecture he gave in Paris after the end of the great war; Sartre, J. (1946) "L'Existentialisme est un Humanisme," Les Editions Nagel. Our philosophy agrees half way with Sartre views of the world that we can be as we decide. A reading selection is "Man Makes Himself," by Jean Paul Sartre, available on the web.

their people into the next chapter of the development of the tribe. What could be the story of America without George Washington, Abraham Lincoln, or Martin Luther King?

If ever humans could choose their parents, the essentialism philosophy of Plato would be founded. Therefore, we come into this world with a purpose, and the Information embedded in our DNA supports this statement. The theory explains that many forget their assignment because of the distraction the material world represents. I didn't discover mine until I went to Ecole Navale. My spiritual calling showed up too early, though. And a seer[11] told me I am a philosopher, the only talent I finally succeeded in saving in my arsenal; the rest slipped through my fingers. The seer made that prophecy while I was still studying economics, having no idea I would go to France the following year.

The material world is full of distractions. As I will delve into it later, Disorder continually impedes the process when Order deploys the Information the individual carries. What if God sends us here to fulfill an assignment? What is God in the first place? Does he need humans?

In the Sartrean existentialist philosophy, one could ask whether man is free and independent from God or dependent, therefore, not free. Anyone who asks the same

---

[11] The general theory of relativity indirectly predicts that all persons are equipped with the ability of see and foresee events, past and future. People who study the light cone of space-time in Minkowski space could understand what I mean. This particular topic could be found in the book "The road to Reality" by the Nobel laureate Sir Penrose; description available in the reference.

question might be erring as the French philosopher himself. God exists but is far from being whatever traditional religions used to depict. We are sure there is no white man with a long white beard in the sky somewhere looking down to punish humans; this is pure fantasy. However, a person exists in the immaterial realm called the Holy Spirit. It is an energy field made of a concatenation of Information and Order. When the field bursts, we call it a spirit; when that spirit is manifested in human flesh, we call it a human spirit.

With the recent development in science, we are tempted to believe that the material universe was created when the system of the immaterial realm moved from a ground state to an excited state. The Belgian priest and physicist George Lemaitre called it the primeval atom[12]. Its instability caused symmetry to break; the field degenerated and exploded or expanded depending on the philosophy of the physicist who interpreted the event. Thus, the material universe was born out of chaos. The presence of Disorder causes space and time to emerge, and the new field, this time, made of a concatenation of information Order, and Disorder provides immaterial particles with mass. Physicists have a special name for this new field and call it the Higgs field, after the British theoretical physicist who set forth the theory.

Do these physicists believe in God? One thing is evident: their works point toward the existence of a God. Sartre rejected God in his philosophy, but I think he was wrong. He would have been an agnostic, and it would be

---

[12] George Lemaitre is one of the founding fathers of modern cosmology and author of the Big Bang theory. His works are listed in the reference.

better. God did indeed give us an essence because our body has functional Information that connotes the existence of a creator or a maker. Science has proved that functional Information exists in living organisms. We cannot say scientists have shot themselves in the foot because science aims to provide a rational explanation for natural phenomena. All their endeavors in recent years have led us closer to the path of an intelligent design behind living organisms on Earth.

Does God exist? As a Christian believer and former minister of God, I believe God exists; as a scientist, I doubt he does not exist; as a philosopher, I can explain how the material world cannot exist without him. Sartre may provide beautiful arguments to reject God, but the universe can never exist without God. Any philosopher who can prove God does not exist must live eternally; here is where I catch tricksters. If you can die, then God exists. The only way to prove God does not exist is to live eternally; by escaping death, one can prove God does not exist because living forever explains the material universe is fundamental. It is death that confirms the existence of God; death is evidence that living organisms are made of flesh and non-flesh entities. The flesh belongs to the material world, and the non-flesh entity emanates from the immaterial realm. The combination of both is called a human being.

Sartre would have been correct in his assertion that God does not exist if he did not die; his death confirms to me that God exists. As an atheist philosopher, Sartre influenced the intellectual scene when the functional Information inside living organisms started to be unraveled; today, I think the French philosopher will struggle to hold his position in a philosophical discussion in front of a knowledgeable audience. The era in which atheists dominate the debate is over, and Sartre was wrong to believe humans have no essence.

Throughout the ages, philosophers and scholars in their works avoid calling the name of God; they try to steer clear of the divine, but in their analyses, the attributes of God are ubiquitous. It seems like nobody can do without it; philosophers cannot develop consistent arguments to explain natural phenomena without invoking this supernatural being. In his book "Being and Nothingness," Sartre also tried hard enough, yet God did not stand far away in his train of thought. To make us swallow the pill, he called the manifestation of this entity nothingness; how can nothingness generate something? Perhaps he had in mind an energy field; John Archibald Wheeler called it "insubstantial nothingness[13]." It's another way of beating around the bush. Some physicists called it a quantum vacuum, a vacuum state that contains no material particles but is filled with energy.

How did the material universe come to be? Sartre never developed any philosophy in this direction but toiled to understand man's place in this material universe. Of course, any philosopher who rejects the presence of God will struggle to explain the origin of the universe. They have strong arguments against believers, though. Usually, they ask, if God is a perfect and whole being as we believe, why did he feel the need to create men?

---

[13] The work of John Wheeler could be found in one of his papers: Wheeler, J. (1989) "Information, Physics, Quantum: The Search for Links."

This question often arises on the lip of philosophers, but they forget that God is love, and love always connotes action. Love is an active verb; love gives, forgives, and serves. If God could love himself, there would be no need to create humans; He creates living organisms to express his love. In the scriptures, God often portrays himself as a river; notice that stagnant water stinks while the flowing river is alive and fresh. A water spring connotes a movement; it flows from a source to the river mouth, emptying itself into the sea.

God needs a material world to express his love. As we said above, life was unstable without the material universe, moving continually from a ground state to an excited state. This instability causes the symmetry to break spontaneously in the primeval atom, giving birth to chaos scientists call entropy. Therefore, space and time emerge as entropy interacts with the concatenation of Information and Order, giving birth to the material universe, which henceforth becomes a safety valve for Heaven.

Without the material world, the immaterial realm is unstable, continually in turmoil, moving from a ground state to an excited state. The quantum vacuum must be an energy field of perfect symmetry filled with immaterial particles that become perturbed. The spontaneous symmetry breaking maintains Order in the immaterial realm because Disorder moves out alongside Information and Order. As Disorder couples with Information and Order, the set gives birth to a new asymmetric field physicist called Higgs field[14]. This latter provides mass to immaterial particles, hence the material world. The advent of the material universe gives stability to Heaven.

Does Heaven need the universe? Not really, but it is necessary for its stability. God does not need humans, but humans are essential for him to be a creator. Sartre chose well the title of his dissertation: "Being and Nothingness." Since Parmenides, scholars have struggled to apprehend these two concepts. Today, we know that Nothingness creates the material universe in which vacuum can be manifested; to make sense of my statement, I should say the immaterial realm begets the material universe in which resides the quantum vacuum. The material universe is made of space-time and matter; the vacuum is a space without any material particles. Nothingness has neither space nor matter; it is an immaterial realm that cannot be stable unless it creates the

---

[14] Peter Higgs, Francois Englert, and Robert Brout wrote a scientific paper in the sixties and theorized that the quantum vacuum was not totally empty. They believed it contains energy and immaterial particles interact with it to acquire mass. They won the Nobel Prize in 2013 after CERN confirmed the mechanism of mass acquisition eventually exists in nature. Their works prove that mass is not a fundamental property, positing the existence of an immaterial realm. The standard model which fundamental theory could be traced back to the gauge theory of Yang-Mills, made physicists labored day and night for almost half a century to finally confirm in 2012 that Heaven exists; that's what they mean in their jargon. Find listed their publications: 1- Higgs, P. (1964) "Broken Symmetries and the Masses of Gauge Bosons," American Physical Society; 2- Englert, F. and Brout, R. (1964) "Broken Symmetry and the Mass of Gauge Vector Mesons," American Physical Society.

material world. In other words, God exists but only finds meaning and essence in humans and the material universe.

Without the material universe, there will be no creation, but God must be a creator; therefore, the universe must be. What we see comes from what cannot be seen; the visible begets the invisible. Thus, the difference between God and humans is found in the Disorder we incorporate into our physical bodies. Both of us are persons made of a concatenation of Information and Order, but we, as human beings, are encased in physical bodies. The Scriptures (2 Corinthians 1:20) said, in Heaven, everything is Yes and Amen, meaning all things are moving in one direction only, but we know Heaven is motionless unless it has a colony. On the other hand, humans express themselves as Yes and NO on Earth, showing two opposite directions in their actions. Entropy separates us from God; religious people call it the devil.

Existence is contingent, but life is not. God does not depend on anything, and nothing causes it to be. It is a field of energy, a concatenation of Information and Order, that will always be eternal and infinite. However, his manifestation is finite and temporal. While existence could be divided into two segments, life is unique. Material existence came to be first, then followed living existence. Humans appear on top and erect themselves as the king of the creation.

I compare human existence to a ship in the sea. A ship requires a captain, and we have one: God made a non-flesh entity to drive the body. This person is free to choose according to certain rules the creator established and promulgated; these laws are known to Christians as the

Decalogue[15]. If the person does not steer his boat, currents and winds will carry him anyway. He has to steer to reach a safe harbor.

Does God fix the end of our lives? Not really, because we have volition and can choose. If God made a young boy a king and this latter jumps off a cliff, he will die and never become a king. As I have said earlier, I was born to be the president of my home country, but I discovered this reality very late, and I have never steered my life in that direction. Is the end fixed in the spiritual realm? Yes, it is fixed because I carry the program in my chromosomes, but I didn't work it out to fruition. Events in the material realm unfold in space and time. Although everything was set up, I also declined to be a pastor and failed to exercise my healing gift; today, I am a philosopher and a theoretical scientist. Our bodies have various ends; we choose which port we want to sail our vessel. Papa Gates wanted his child to become a lawyer, but the young Bill opted for computer science and made it successfully and happily.

According to the Bahamian pastor Myles Monroe, God has a program for each of us, and he calls his plan a work; on the other hand, our parents or society also have a plan for us and call it a job. Monroe believed the individual is satisfied in his work rather than his job. Thus, each individual must toil to lay hands on his program to get into his work. Life is working hard to break away from this planet; the purpose of

---

[15] We elucidate this topic in one of our articles in philosophy available on ssrn.com, an Elsevier repository for scientific and philosophical research. The paper is free to download; here is the link: Zanou, A. (2022) "On Morality?" Social Science Research Network [Elsevier]

life is to scatter throughout the universe, and God is using humans to achieve that goal. Therefore, he equips each individual coming on Earth to work on his assignment. All achievers, engineers, scientists, inventors, and spiritual leaders have been working in the field of God without knowing it. It doesn't matter what the individual believes; he moils unbeknownst to him. That's how Francis Crick worked on the program of the DNA molecules to unravel the existence of functional Information behind living organisms. Today, his works have become a pivotal step in understanding the origin of life; this man killed Darwinism because we know evolution was not random but directed. As Richard Dawkins put it during a conversation with Jim Al-Khalili:" Natural Selection is clever than you are[16]." He was right because Natural selection is a program, and whatever is clever cannot be random.

The same God used Professor Yuval Noah Harari to demonstrate how humans gained ascendency over the rest of the animals. Science still doesn't know why one group of primates stood upright, but Professor Harari explained why and how the Sapiens succeeded in dominating the world. By proving humans are equipped with a frequency of imagination, he also confirmed that intuition exists alongside, making the human mind a transceiver. If we can transmit signals, we can also receive them. Imagination and intuition make it possible for humans to operate their minds efficiently through faith. The achiever receives a signal,

---

[16] Professor Dawkins uttered those words during a conversation around his previous book "Science in the Soul: Selected Writings of a Passionate Rationalist." Here is the link to the conversation: https://www.youtube.com/watch?v=735o-d62FGE&t=179s

believes in it, and uses his imagination to fine-tune his vision, and then he sets himself to work and reach a result.

That's how the American engineer John Bardeen invented the transistor so that Bill Gates could revolutionize microcomputers, allowing Elon Musk and Jeff Bezos to amass a fortune to engage in the space program. Everything is connected; nothing is random, as Darwinians have always taught. All these people work for the energy field we call God; they are just unaware of it. Sometimes, God convinces people that he does not exist so that they may think they are working of their own volition. Humans long to be independent, and we are. If humans know they are working to help life break away from Earth, they will lose enthusiasm. If CERN physicists knew God existed, they wouldn't have moiled day and night to confirm the existence of the Higgs mechanism in nature. Does this make God a manipulator? No! Far from it, God does not manipulate anyone since he does not intervene directly in the business of atheists.

People who believe in God see him at work in their lives. Of course, God is present in each of us as a concatenation of Information and Order. Who can step forward and claim he has no Information in his body? Anyone alive has a portion of God in him; the non-flesh entity comprises Information and Order; the body is made of Information, Order, and Disorder. The non-flesh lives inside the flesh as a captain sits on the bridge to steer his ship.

All non-flesh entities come from the same source. That's where the imbroglio of life stems from; people don't know we are all made of the same stuff. North and South Koreans, as did the Hutu and Tutsi in Rwanda, never knew they were brothers. Had the Russians and the Ukrainians known they were made of the same stuff, they wouldn't have been killing each other. In the allegory of the water tower, I describe the manifestation of human life as follows:

"Life is a giant water tower set on top of a hill to serve the city down in the valley. The water comes down through a central pipe and branches out. Each branch has a filter upon which the Engineer installs a pump dispenser with various flavors in small flasks. An additional device could alter the temperature of the fluid as it runs out of the faucet. Hence, water comes out with an apple taste for some, a mango taste, pineapple, orange, grape, watermelon, cherry, lime, and lemon. Some individuals could get it hot, fresh, or cold. The Russians and the Ukrainians don't know the same water is flowing through their faucets, but we know it is the same water for everybody.

I have seen people who have passion fruit taste in freshwater and yet hang themselves. I have also seen some with a lemon taste, running out hot, but they add sugar and ice to it and make lemonade with ingenuity. Whatever the individual makes with her water is up to her; one can drink it as it comes or add some ingredients. This allegory explains why humans are equipped with creativity; animals don't have choices.

A lion has never built a weapon; it relies on its God-given armor: powerful jaws and teeth. Humans build tools; unfortunately, they have also made atomic bombs to trap themselves. We are equipped with a creative mind to make our stay on this planet comfortable. Life can only achieve its purpose if humans survive and prosper on Earth. Some people believe humans will scatter throughout the universe, departing from the Earth. On balance, humans need to be creative, and our daughters must not be left behind.

Mary Wollstonecraft, in her epoch, already considered how the education system was flawed and set up to disadvantage women. Today, things have changed; no one can wait to be taught; libraries are open and readily available in almost every city in modern countries. We change the world through knowledge and understanding; our ancestors have chosen the path of knowledge, and we must be good at it.

Life is supportive of its project; it does not abandon humans on their own. Our daughters need to be aware of life's method to push its agenda forward. As we always say, existence is the manifestation of life. Living existence was possible through Information; first came Information to assemble molecules and atoms in an orderly manner; that's how life emerged on Earth. Wollstonecraft believed women, in common with men, are placed on this Earth to develop their abilities. For that cause, I will not sidle with the subject; I must delve into this phenomenon to open the understanding of our daughters on the topic of scientific achievement.

Information is still behind everything life does to promote its agenda, and humans, the conscious agents in the service of life, acquire their knowledge in two fundamental ways: instruction and revelation. By instruction, I mean schooling, apprenticeship, observation, experiment, and any kind of transfer that does not involve voices emanating from the unknown realm. Humans interact with the physical environment, but worlds unseen to their eyes exist. All that exists is not what we can see; worlds spread beyond our perception. When signals come from these unseen realms, we call it a revelation. Thus, revelation is the second way by which humans acquire knowledge. By revelation, I mean intuition and dreaming. All achievers reach a result, a goal, or an invention through one of these channels.

For instance, Carl Benz saw his horseless carriage in his mind, believed in his vision, and worked hard to bring it to fruition. August Kekulé discovered the formula of Benzene through a dream. Often, people neglect their dreams or visions because they think their mind is hallucinating. These people never understand that unknown worlds surround us; it's hard to swallow, but that is the reality. Animals don't see at the same frequency range as humans; some can read into the ultraviolet and infrared. Eyes in the animals' kingdom come in various sizes and shapes. By adjusting their lenses in a particular manner, some animals can penetrate different wavelengths of the spectrum; humans don't know how to do that. It is pure ignorance to affirm all that exists is what we see; we perceive less than one percent of what is present.

Today, the brawl between scientists and religious people is the cause of our trouble; the unceasing fight between religion and science sometimes pushes scientists to deny the undeniable. To thwart religionists' agenda, scientists are obliged to shovel materialism into our throats, although the blatant evidence that matter is not fundamental. Scientists know the material world is not fundamental because matter and energy are not equal but equivalent. Energy is converted and stored in matter; this fact confirms the famous formula of Albert Einstein. CERN scientists also confirm that mass is not a fundamental property.

Scientists are slow to understand that they cannot achieve any scientific result without using faith. Faith is not only a religious term but also the way the mind functions. Our daughters must grasp the mechanism by which the mind operates. Usually, people confound faith and beliefs; they are not the same things. A belief is an acceptance of something to be true without necessarily proving it. It is exclusively related to religion, while faith is fundamental. Faith is one way the human mind works. Anyone who uses his creative mind efficiently is already into faith. No researcher could reach a result without using faith. All scientists use faith without knowing it.

If our daughters want to get into the scientific arena, they must understand that revelation is better than instruction. People who change the world do so with novel ideas, which come to the individual, whether through dreaming or intuition. When the individual receives the vision, she must believe it; if she doesn't, she will not be able to put herself to work. One must accept whatever she sees in her mind; that is the definition of faith. The scriptures define faith as a conviction of things not seen. Therefore, the individual must admit that realms spread beyond the physical world. Our vision limits us to one world; we don't perceive the source where life originates from; we are accustomed to where life manifests itself. Hence, life and its manifestation are not the same things.

To sum up, life is manifested as existence on planet Earth; it emanates from the immaterial realm, a perfect symmetry, while the material universe has asymmetry; that's why the manifestation of life is possible in the material. If symmetry hadn't broken in the immaterial realm, the universe would have never existed; the spontaneous symmetry breaking in the original energy field caused the universe to emerge. Material existence occurred in the first position, followed by living existence which is divided into two kingdoms according to the classification of the Swedish Botanist Von Linnaeus. Humans branched out through the animal kingdom and climbed to the top to become the king of the creation.

Life is what we cannot fully understand, but existence is within our ken. Anything that exists must be located in space, traceable through time, and possess mass. In contrast with presence, existence is confined to the material universe only.

A human being is made of a non-flesh entity encased in a physical body. His existence can spread over 120 years in this modern society, according to the preventive medicine doctor Frederic Saldmann. The individual sojourns in a woman's womb and comes into existence after forty weeks of gestation. Her life out of the womb is divided between training sessions and solo sessions. The first session runs from birth to twenty-one years old and could be divided into three ages: the age of assimilation, the age of reason, and the age of consciousness.

Once the individual reaches maturity at twenty one, she is called to proclaim her independence to secede from the parental house to start a solo life. For that cause, she must perform the self-awareness operation to know herself and discover her dominant program. She must also make two fundamental decisions about her future: be celibate or be in partnership; reproduce or preserve her body. These choices help her find a genuine partner to make the journey more comfortable in the solo session. Life in this session is hinged on two fundamental pillars: work and relationship. Challenges, timing, and investment characterize this period of the individual's life. While the young girl's clock ticks against her, the boy must invest wisely in his life to make it successful. The two individuals constitute the unit of production and are assigned a specific function in the marital house. For that cause, both must understand and be aware of each other's constitution; they are called to live in the marital home as a man and woman, a husband and wife, or, broadly speaking, as a pilot and copilot.

Second Distinction: Man and Woman

I could not disagree with you when noticing that humanity truly is male and that men define "woman." Not only do men define women, but they also set up their standard of beauty. In human society, men define beauty and impose the ideal on women. Thus, most women struggle to fit in. As you have always insinuated, the problem of women has always been a problem of men.

I will not refrain from delving into the differentiation of man and woman. I brushed it earlier, and now I am set to comb through the topic. The source of everything is unique, but the manifestation has differentiation. Think about a river, for instance. It sprouts from a mountain and meanders gently through the land, where it bifurcates according to obstacles on its way. Man and woman have similar essences: one life but a different existence. A man is a unique way life manifests itself, and a woman is another way life expresses itself. Can we say the man comes first? Not really, because both man and woman exist in the original hermaphroditic being. In the Symposium, Plato describes the hermaphrodite[17] as male and female in one body with four arms, four legs, and two heads. The creature has both male and female parts. Thus united, it has authority and

---

[17] The idea of hermaphroditic beings was discussed in the symposium in the speech Aristophanes gave after he recovered from his hiccups.

power, but the gods became angry at their rebellion and halved them down into males and females.

This particular story is in the book of Genesis in the Bible, where God created the first human as male and female. The creator took a lump of clay from the ground and formed a body. He breathed a breath of life inside his creation, and the clay became a living being. As the rebellion loomed, the creator caused a deep sleep in his creature and separated it into man and woman.

Science confirms that all living organisms on Earth emerge from a single cell. Life has a single entry point into this material universe, evolving to yield the biodiversity we see today. Without any doubt, we can say humans crown the evolutionary process because humans have a frequency of personhood which confers them a personality.

As you mentioned, women didn't think independently without men in the erstwhile society. They lived in the shadow of men because life was found in the state of nature. The subjugation of women in the human species was due to religion and the misinterpretation of the ancient texts. However, we can find a rational explanation for the phenomenon. Male humans are more muscular and physically built than the females. Notice that several species have their females larger than the males in the animal kingdom. Many insects, birds, and some mammals have their females more considerable than the males. That's the case of spotted hyenas and whales, for instance. Researchers let us know that in these species, matriarchy is imposed because the animal world is a Darwinian system. It is the law of the stronger that prevails. Everything is solved by physical force. In his masterpiece Leviathan, the British philosopher Thomas Hobbes said that life is solitary, poor, nasty, brutish, and short in the state of nature[18]; that type of existence is not designed for women because they lack the physical strength to deal with it. The archaic condition of war of all against all is not a suitable environment for women to thrive.

If matriarchy is imposed in the animal kingdom whenever the females are larger than the males, can we say patriarchy is established whenever the males are more physically considerable? To our knowledge, we can say that science confirms such a phenomenon. We must not forget that humans are also animals, and the difference between humans and animals is that we have the frequency of personhood that gives us personalities. And whenever we fail to live by principles, instinct will surface and govern our lives.

We didn't live by principles in the olden days, and our history is there to prove it. The Vikings didn't live by principles; they killed and looted cities they invaded. Are women qualified to face such violence? I say no! You are a woman, and you know it. When the German soldiers invaded France during the Second World War, men didn't stay at home and sent women to the front.

In the state of nature, humans don't live by principles but by instinct. Humans become animals and behave like beasts to prevail. We know that when consciousness

---

[18] Hobbes discussed the state of nature in the first part of the book, in section XIII: Of the Natural Condition of Mankind as Concerning Their Felicity and Misery.

is projected on the screen of the mind, women have a beautiful Representation of the world, and they see harmony and beauty, while men perceive chaos and violence. We live according to what we see in our minds. Notice that correctional facilities are not crowded with women; they are filled with men. It is one blatant proof that men are more wicked than women and often perceive chaos. Life is always mental; that's why people enter vegetative states if the mind fails to operate correctly. Nobody can live without a mind because life is mental. We live according to the internal film that unfolds in our minds.

Yuval Noah Harari said humans control the world because they live in a dual reality while animals live objectively. Of course, we do because we are subjects with personalities living in objects. Our objective reality is related to our physical body, and our fictional reality is linked to our personalities, things animals don't have. We gain ascendancy over the rest of the animals because our fictional reality works. Why does Professor Harari call it a fictional reality? Is it truly unreal? The Information embedded in our DNA tells us that it is not. There is always an author behind every piece of information designed to achieve a goal. And the most fundamental principle inside our body is known as the decalogue. The love of humans summarizes everything about humans. We live in a chaotic world because nobody lives by principles anymore.

As I have said earlier, a human being is a spirit that lives in a body, has a soul, and operates with a mind. The spirit is located in the heart, the soul in the blood, and the mind in the brain. The spirit, soul, and mind are electromagnetic fields hovering over these organs. In concatenation, they form what religious people call the inward-man; Arthur Schopenhauer identified it as a will-to-life. Indeed, there is an energy that powers the human body, and we die when that energy leaks out. Whenever the boundary fence that protects the energy breaches, it starts leaking out, causing the body systems to lose balance. Death occurs when the system formed by synthesis and degradation loses its balance in the body. And both men and women die in the same way.

The body dies in two fundamental ways: sudden loss of synchronicity and gradual loss of synchronicity. Death does not distinguish men from women; both die in a similar pattern, but the statistics show that women live longer than men. It is so because women tend to manage their entropy better than men, who love taking risks. Human history records that women are often confined to the house while men venture out to hunt and seek food. You ask in your book, where does the submission of women come from?

History never reported a war between man and woman. I can also reassure you that woman submission does not come from God, although the idea originates from the Bible. Humans often misinterpret ancient scriptures, and since men set themselves up to be the guardians of the traditional values, man erected himself as One, and woman became the Other. But before the era of religion, the state of nature conferred man the first position and put woman behind. In the beginning, it was not a big deal because the first position was not so glamorous. Remember, Hobbes said life in the state of nature is solitary, poor, nasty, brutish, and short. I could guarantee you that even if the first position was offered to women, they would have declined it. Life was not pleasant in the state of nature and less occupying the first position. The war has just broken up in Ukraine, and I can guarantee you that women would not come forward and send men to safety; it's the opposite we have seen.

I understand your inquiries and share your concerns about the subjugation of women, the Jews, and the Blacks, as you mentioned throughout the book. The circumstances were different, and history could help us. While the Jews and the Blacks were the minority, women were always equal to men, yet they came second. The Jews and the Blacks were subjugated by force while women yielded to men by love. Between man and woman, it has always been a story of love. Both are made to be together. They are the two sides of the same coin.

The relationship between man and woman is part of the natural law. The subjugation of women is a misinterpretation of the natural law, which Jesus reinstated by demonstrating the relationship between master and servants. On the night he was arrested, the scriptures reported that Jesus got up from the meal, took off his clothes, and girded himself with a towel. Then he poured water into a basin, washed his apostles' feet, and dried them with the towel. After he had finished washing their feet, he put on his clothes and returned to his place. And he said unto them:

"Do you understand what I have done for you?" he asked them. "You call me 'Teacher' and 'Lord,' and rightly so, for that is what I am. Now that I, your Lord and Teacher, have washed your feet, you also should wash one another's feet. I have set you an example that you should do as I have done for you."

The relationship between man and woman is a business of love. The leader loves the servant by washing her feet. The only moment man is One and woman is the Other is when the man washes the feet of the woman. Man and woman are two halves riveted to each other to be whole and fulfill the purpose of life. They were halved down because of the upcoming rebellion. The esoteric interpretation of the Bible said God divided the original human's absolute authority and spread it into two separate bodies to prevent the rebels from seizing power. It worked because, after the rebellion, the insurgents could not use the power that was kept separate. A man alone cannot procreate; both need each other to perpetuate the species and fulfill the purpose of life.

The first humans seceded from the kingdom of heaven and proclaimed their independence. Since then, man started alienating woman. He relegated her to the second position and conferred her the role of reproduction and housewife. Biology also played a critical role in the demise of woman. The chaos that followed the secession opened their eyes. The spiritual entity was dead inside, and the only thing left was the physical body, which gave the man some advantage. Man, by definition, is taller and more robust than a woman. Thus, the relation man-woman turned into the benefit of men in every society. Life in the state of nature is about physical strength. Honestly, the woman is not qualified to play that game. She is the essence of love, the guardian of life, not a killer. That's why armies and police forces worldwide are composed essentially of men and not women. And most criminals are men because the carceral population is made mostly of men and not women.

I do not think that women complained as much about their situation in the past as they do today. In the same way enslaved people usually did not complain much about their lifestyle, women didn't see anything wrong. Moreover, religion justified the situation, blaming humanity's fall upon women, so women resigned and accepted their fate.

The world is not designed to be divided between man and woman because they are complementary beings condemned to be together. They are joint heirs of God and co-equal to administer the estate. If we don't perceive things that way, serious trouble may arise between our sons and daughters. Today, feminists see domination while women in the erstwhile society admit the situation. The diffusion of knowledge has played a crucial role in the emancipation of women. Your compatriot Olympe de Gouges, beheaded during the French Revolution, said in her pamphlet:

"Woman, wake up; the tocsin of reason is being heard throughout the whole universe; discover your rights. The powerful empire of nature is no longer surrounded by prejudice, fanaticism, superstition, and lies. The flame of truth has dispersed all the clouds of folly and usurpation."

My Dear Simone, I am afraid that you interpret the duality of the sexes as a conflictual situation. Unlike other dualism, man and woman are far away from being opposite. They complete and complement each other. It is an abuse of language when we compare man and woman with other dualism expressed as an antagonism. Hot and cold cancel each other; light absorbs darkness, but man and woman unite and reproduce. There has never been a war between man and woman. The two individuals have always been in love with each other; it is a story of love between them. The world has always belonged to men because we have always lived in the state of nature. Things will change when women begin to raise their kids differently to have mature and wise men in power. You lived through the Second World War and experienced the German invasion. Did you tell men of Paris to run to safety while women took weapons to fight? It was the opposite, I presumed. It has always been the opposite. During wars, men grab weapons and tell women to run to safety. That's why the world has always been in the hands of men. The problem of man and woman will end if we perceive the situation differently. As you nicely put it in the introduction of the first volume, I quote:

"To see clearly, one needs to get out of these ruts; these vague notions of superiority, inferiority, and equality that have distorted all discussions must be discarded in order to start anew."

The white man has created a world of division, and when some men notice their mediocrity, they hurry to demean the minority to feel comfortable. You said it well, "the most mediocre of males believe himself a demigod next to a woman." We must not fall into the trap and miss the point. Man and woman are complementary entities; there is no way we can compare them. When working together, a rotor and a stator have meaning; otherwise, they are meaningless and insignificant parts ready to be ditched. Science said we share more than ninety-nine percent of our genome in common; only 0.1% makes the difference from one individual to another. Our differences are negligible, yet we have been taught and led to focus on them more than our similarities.

The Hegelian idea of active and passive when referring to males and females is not erroneous. As I have earlier said, we need to pay attention to how we perceive the world to avoid missing the point. As you know, the penis fits into the vagina, and during sexual intercourse, the male empties himself inside the woman. Engineers produce electricity by rotating the rotor inside a stator. There is nothing pejorative about it. I am from Africa, and I have dark skin; it does not make me less human as the white man had portrayed it in the past. Feminists must refrain from incendiary statements that could lead the youth astray.

Feminism has lost its original meaning because of bald assertions and mischievous thinking. It is a fact that the male represents the active part of the force, but he is unstable. The female is the passive side and stable; that's why men need women and vice versa. Life would be unable to reach its purpose unless both individuals stay together. Women have a lot of values we must teach our daughters; they are not inferior. We don't need to proceed like mediocre males who continually feel insecure and run after subterfuge to denigrate women to be comfortable. Women don't need to put men down as men used to do. The fight of feminists must not be to pay evil by evil; that's how some feminists have changed the movement. They want to live and do as men do. Nowadays, some get drunk and sleep around. Some also want to rob banks and do naughty things as men do. And some of them are paying alimony.

Women are the guardians of life, and even some female species can reproduce without the males; it is called parthenogenesis. That's to show how valuable females are in the manifestation of life. Nature expects great things from women, and they must not allow mediocre men to distract them. Mediocre men depict women as the abomination of the creation; I see them as nature's masterpieces. Since I understood existence, my panegyric on women made men accuse me wrongly, but I remain a fervid defender of women, and we must focus on reality in our fight. Women must not become men and do stupid things as men do.

As you have noticed, the sperm is active and designed for mobility; it moves toward the egg that passively waits for it to begin the fertilization process. Like the female who receives the male inside her during copulation, the egg also welcomes the sperm. And the two gametes merge and unite instead of canceling each other out. It shows that both man and woman are complementary beings, and they need each other. There is no man apart from a woman; they exist together as human beings to perpetuate the human species. That's how we must tell the story of humans to our children. And after forty weeks of gestation, a new human being is born, made of a physical body in which the non-flesh entity penetrates to vitalize it.

Anyone familiar with petroleum refineries knows oil refining is an industrial process in which heated crude oil is transformed into various useful products such as fuel oil, diesel, kerosene, gasoline, propane, and butane. The refined products are recuperated according to the temperature in the distillation tower. We have a similar process in the body, except that spirit, soul, and mind are defined according to the vibrational frequency instead of temperature. At birth, the non-flesh entity that penetrates the body is carried to the lungs by the first breath; it reaches the heart by the blood and later arrives in the brain. The electromagnetic field it generates over the heart is known as the spirit; the field hovering over the blood is called the soul, and the activity over the brain is the mind. The three fields collapse into one at death and are generally known as spirit. After the body's demise, we can no longer talk about a soul or mind but a spirit, which is nothing more than a particular electromagnetic spectrum frequency. Technically, the mind and the soul are only related to the body; the physical body differentiates them. People use them interchangeably, but it is okay.

Notice that after death is pronounced, several body organs remain useful for up to twenty-four hours. Physicians can reuse the heart only within four hours; while the mitochondria are still functional in this organ, death was pronounced, proving life does not emanate from the mitochondria as materialist scientists believe. Life comes to the body by the non-flesh entity the newborn picks up in his first breath. The person, made of a concatenation of Information and Order, is pure energy different from the physical body. Thus, human life starts at birth, or to be more accurate, the individual's existence begins at conception, but his life commences when he picks up the first breath at birth.

To summarize what I have said earlier, humans are spiritual beings, and the spirit has no gender identity. By definition, the spirit which is encased in a male body is called a man. The one that vitalizes a female temple is called a woman. This non-flesh entity in its expression pulls the woman into immanence but pushes the man into transcendence. These two manifestations are antipodals; there is no antinomy. For that cause, a specific body is designed to match each person's respective functions. The human body, in general, has many symmetries; I should say chiralities, to be more precise, but the male and the female external organs are complementary. A man is physically dense but emotionally unstable; a woman is stable but physically less muscular than a man. Their respective hormones determine their degree of stability. The testosterone makes the man unstable, while oxytocin provides stability to the woman. By stability, we intend to measure and appreciate the individual's position regarding justice, love, and peace. Men score poorly; they populate the correctional facilities.

A man is a system of immaterial components that pilots a male body. A woman is a system that controls a female body. Sometimes, the body could come out of the womb ambiguous. Some individuals are born with some issues, and the medical staff cannot decide if the baby is a male or female at first glance. This ambiguity is known as intersex or androgyny. This ambivalence puts in shambles the sexuality of the individuals as they grow up, generating the spectrum we know today as LGBTQ. I will go through this phenomenon in the next section if I have enough time. However, I have to point out that sex refers to the individual's biological characteristics, mainly focusing on the physical body. The manifestation of immaterial components determines gender: either the man dominates in the male body, or the woman gains ascendency in the female body; these are the most commonly known genders. The non-flesh entity has no gender identity, meaning it is both man and woman; how do we know that? Every individual on earth has both male and female hormones in his body systems. As I already mentioned, when complications occur, the immaterial components struggle to pronounce themselves in the body systems; in that case, the man comes up in the female body, and a woman dominates in the male body.

Same-sex attraction occurs when the man rising inside the female body craves a female body, although the individual has female genitalia. The woman dominating a male body will also desire a male, although the individual has a male sex organ. In general rule, we know males crave a female body and vice versa; the same rule applies to homosexuality. The change emanates from the inner-system of the individuals. The phenomenon is still complex, and science struggles to grasp it, but we know entropy plays a significant role in this mess.

People often say gender is a social construct, which is absurd because individuals make society; individual humans exist first before gathering together to create a community. The question is similar to the notorious egg and chicken puzzle. If individuals exist first, then gender cannot be a social construct because men and women have penises and vaginas before bonding to create a community. It is not society that decides women should get pregnant; Nature does. Nature gives them a womb and puts two voluminous breasts on their chest, causing them to operate in immanence. I am against gender roles, though. Consciousness has evolved, and society must grow accordingly.

Currently, gender is a national debate and television news in the United States. Many believe it is a social construct; let's clarify the situation: if these people are talking about the English word "gender," then it's not a social construct. Perhaps they might be talking about another word or slang; I don't know. However, the English word gender comes from the French "gendre," which derives from the verb "engendrer," meaning to beget or to father. Gender always connotes genes or generation and is more complex than sex. It is all the time related to birth or giving birth. There is always something to produce with gender. With gender, we must bear in mind seed and soil to incubate. And we know the male shoots the seed, and the female receives and incubates it to produce more of its kinds. The male produces sperm, which he gives to the female, who uses it to reproduce a baby. From that perspective, we can agree that we have two significant pools of gender. Apart from the two most popular genders, masculine and feminine, we have a spectrum between them; science says these individuals are 1.7% of the world population, which is not negligible. This spectrum depends on the whims of the entropy and how it interacts with the immaterial components during the gestation period.

As gender has become a heated topic, the question "what is a woman" has eluded many experts. Since a human being is a concatenation of a non-flesh entity and a physical body, gender refers to the non-flesh entity, and sex connotes the physical body. Notice that there is a difference between a woman and a female; biologists often describe female thinking they define a woman. Humans are not solely flesh. Although the evidence, many still believe we are flesh; we are more than that. The expression of the non-flesh entity in the body as woman causes the body system to secrete more oxytocin. At the same time, man drives the body systems to produce more testosterone. Thus, a woman is a non-flesh entity that dominates a female body. To be a woman, the person must be expressed as woman in a female body. If the non-flesh entity shows up as man in a female body, the individual is not a woman; in the same way, the expression of woman in a male body is not a woman. These individuals fall into the spectrum category, a phenomenon we know is caused by the interaction of the entropy in the body, whether at birth or during pregnancy.

Our daughters cannot remain ignorant of the five categories of individuals that roam our planet. We classify these individuals according to birth, upbringing, the degree of their entropy, and how they manage it. But, before we reach there, let us shine some light on the internal chaos that defines the individuals.

Entropy is the unrest in the body systems that increases with age. That degradation in the body is hooked with synthesis, which maintains it within a controllable range. We sleep to lower the level of degradation in the body; thus, chaos in the body is low in the morning after a restful night. It is low in the child and high in the adult, growing bigger until the body loses its management and death follows. When people become unable to manage and control it, death occurs. Entropy interferes with our emotions and helps define our personalities. Whether the individual becomes a thief, a killer, a bully, a rapist, a gentleman, or a peacemaker depends on the entropy's level and how the individual succeeds in managing it.

The entropy is low in women and high in men because of testosterone, which characterizes men. Testosterone is the primary hormone among the entropy hormones. Along with cortisol, epinephrine, and norepinephrine, they determine the entropy inside the body. Testosterone level in humans helps distinguish three different classes if we take one unit as the lowest level possible and ten as the highest we could find. Class one is primarily composed of women; they upgrade to class two by the time they get engaged and start living as a couple. Men are in class three and downgrade to class two when they settle or become a father.

Class three individuals are agitated, craving sex all day long; there is nothing wrong with them. Our daughters need to be aware of this phenomenon to navigate it correctly. Since testosterone helps define the classes of entropy, and this internal chaos shapes our personality, how the individual manages his unrest is significant in society. Our daughters need to know what is going on in the minds of men. Most of them have high entropy; therefore, they have a chaotic Representation as consciousness is projected on the screen of the mind. Men don't perceive reality as women do. Men often go to war because they have such Representation in their minds in the first place. Life is mental; nobody goes to war unless he conceives it and justifies it in his mind. Women don't rely on their muscles, so their perception does not focus on fights. Biology is at play here.

One thing is to have a chaotic Representation, and another is to yield to one's impulses. Women are stable because they have a beautiful Representation of the world, while men see chaos. Here is an example I would like to submit to your judgment. I want you to tell me which one between man and woman is capable of committing the following crime. Give me your assessment, please:

When I was still a truck driver traveling from state to state in America, I took a break at a small truck stop not far from Las Vegas. It was a sunny day, and a few trucks were in the parking lot when I pulled over. Ten minutes later, a commercial vehicle pulled over in the shade in front of me. The driver got off and walked to the gas station. He went into the shop for his thirty-minute break. A few minutes after he left, I spotted an individual erring on the premises. I could say a jaywalker or wanderer who had nothing to do with his day. For some reason, the individual stopped between the tractor and the trailer. He looked around to see if nobody was watching. He bent over slightly and pulled the kingpin to disconnect the mechanism that hooked the trailer to the tractor. And he walked away.

When the driver returned from his break, he got into his truck and pulled forward. The trailer suddenly fell with a deafening noise. The driver stopped and got out of his vehicle to consider the damage. He crossed his two hands over his head in total despair.

According to you, what could be the identity of this thug? Could this mugger be a man or a woman?

If you think this jaywalker was a man, you are right. Women often see harmony and beauty in the world. To recall your memory, when the heart pumps blood to the brain, consciousness is projected on the screen of the mind as Will and Representation. In the Will, we have Desire governed by Reason. In the Representation, we have Memory and Perception. Here is where the difference between man and woman starts; everything begins in their minds. The probability of having a woman commit such a crime is very low. Men commit crimes without any apparent motive; women don't. The statistics show that most female serial killers[19] have a strong alibi and gain something from their crimes. They don't act aimlessly.

Males often commit crimes without any rational aim. In many serial killers I studied, some seduced the woman and got everything they wanted, and at the end, killed their victims who sometimes had already fallen in love with them. Female serial killers often target dying older people; they swindle their money or fool these seniors into bequeathing their assets and then killing them. Money is often the motivation of women, but males can kill for nothing.

Our daughters must understand the physiology of men to handle them efficiently. We can distinguish five categories of men on this planet according to their conception, upbringing, and how they manage to control their entropy.

Category 1: People conceived with affection, raised in love, and find love.

Category 2: People conceived without affection, raised without love, but succeed in finding love.

Category 3: People conceived without affection, raised without love, and have failed to find love but succeeded in finding a genuine way to deal with their entropy.

---

[19] The following document gives a glimpse into female serial killing: Frei, A., Völlm, B., Graf, M. and Dittmann, V. (2006) "Female serial killing: review and case report," Criminal Behavior and Mental Health-Wiley Online Library

Category 4: People conceived with affection, raised in love, but somehow fail to find love and a genuine way to deal with their entropy.

Category 5: People who were conceived without affection and raised without love. In addition, they grew up and failed to find love and a genuine way to deal with their entropy.

People in categories four and five made up the majority of the carceral population. It's home to dictators, terrorists, murderers, robbers, and criminals of all kinds. They have no clue what love is; their hearts have hardened over time, becoming insensitive to human suffering. As society often confounds love with lust and self-love, the population could believe these people are in love, but the reality is different. We often hear people say stupid things like love can make you commit a crime; that's not love. Love gives, forgives, and serves. A dictator who kills a quarter of his population to please a woman is not in love; he is mad. The adage says a person who is nice to you but rude to the waiter is not a nice person. Love heals; it changes our stone hearts into flesh. Even in front of your enemies, love never seeks vengeance. Does anyone want to understand love? Study Jesus, the epitome of love. I will come back later on this topic of love, which often eludes humans.

Like traumatized feminists who create trouble out of thin air, men of categories four and five are difficult to deal with; our daughters must be aware of it. These men often lack empathy and would not make good husbands. Empathy is the ability to project oneself into the other to feel whatever the fellow is experiencing. For instance, a husband who comes from work to claim a dinner while his wife curls up in pain on the couch has no sense of empathy. A good husband must seek to understand the situation and show kindness to assist his wife in such a condition. He must be flexible enough to run the house and care for the kids at that particular moment. Men who cannot manage their entropy often fail to be good partners; they chronically lack oxytocin, the hormone that brings harmony to women. Biology plays a significant role in distinguishing man from woman.

Men must understand that women are sometimes sick and indisposed due to their natural conditions. That's why both men and women must get to know each other before tying the knot. I will not let our daughters be ignorant about these facts. A woman's physiology brings upon her some undesirable situations, disrupting her sexuality. Unlike men, who remain constant with their libido through the month, women have three seasons in their sexuality.

I call the first season Wet season. It is the moment women long for sex without any external stimuli. The body of a woman secretes mucous and lubricates the vagina's canal. The individual has nothing to do with it because the phenomenon escapes her control. Things unfold on themselves as the program is already embedded inside women's chromosomes and unfolds on itself. They discover its manifestation and can only assist as a spectator. However, women who pay attention to their bodies could gather many clues and avoid being surprised by the event. It is not good for a woman to be surprised by a pregnancy since you label it a curse. Women must make an effort and join their partners in their adventure so that they may become aware of this particular manifestation of Nature. A woman must be able to identify her ovulation window because she carries the burden of gestation. The closer women get to the ovulation date, the stronger the sexual urge.

The second season is the Recovery season. The body manages the unfortunate situation. The woman's body prepared for a feast, but things did not work out properly as the system had desired. Life continually inveigles us to copulate and reproduce. The egg will not be fertilized if no sperm comes at the rendezvous. The Recovery season helps the body systems control the disappointment. This season is a period of mitigation for women as their bodies manage the failure. The woman's body systems always compute the Recovery season as a failure.

The last season, which is the third one, is called the Dry season. It is the moment women bleed out. The body systems get rid of the nest made for the fetus. The nest was built with blood tissues and protected by some particular hormones. At the end of the Recovery season, when the body finally notices that things will never work out, it sheds off the nest, which evacuates through the vagina as menstruation. After the Dry season follows the Wet season, and the cycle starts over again until women reach menopause, the moment the ovaries are out of stock. Women's hormones fluctuate accordingly, causing their moods to swing.

As you wrote, the woman is more emotional; she may be irritable than usual with serious psychological problems, but notice that Nature does not send her away from the house. Natural Selection chooses the man and sends him outside to fight for food. Every time we move out from the natural perspective of things, we may err and commit mistakes. Man and woman could be described as an object and its shadow (anyone who thinks the man is the object and the woman the shadow has already a problem); they are the reality of the same coin. There is no way we can dissociate them. Men have done horrible things in the past, but the time has come to move forward and educate our children differently. Not every woman thinks her body is an alienated opaque thing in which a stubborn and foreign life makes and unmakes a crib every month. Our daughters will believe whatever we tell them, so we must strive to show them reality instead of fiction. Pregnancy is not a curse, at least not for those women who choose reproduction because there is nothing more beautiful in this existence than having kids and transferring one's knowledge to them. Well-prepared mothers love their kids and desire to spend time with them. Some women don't even want to let their children go as they come of age.

Pregnancy is part of woman's psychology and physiology. Do you think trees complain about blossoming and bearing fruit? We cherish trees that bear fruit; we prune them and pray they may bear more fruit the following season. Humans are the only species that complain about their conditions, which, unfortunately, they toil day and night to worsen. Our ideologies and doctrines do not make things better for us; they complicate life and make our existence even more miserable.

I admit that gestation is tiring work; that's why I always say our daughters must not get pregnant for free. Do women truly understand that pregnancy is exhausting? If they do, they will choose their man carefully. They must get pregnant with a man who asks and desires a kid. Gestation becomes a nightmare when the man has never asked for it and doesn't want to hear anything.

A woman is not an error of nature; she is the real human being, the mother of all men roaming the planet. I think you have exaggerated when displaying the physiology and psychology of women as a catastrophe. I disagree with your conclusion when you believe women's subordination to the species causes these characteristics, which you spread out in the first part of the book. Women are designed to play specific roles in a complex system, men as well. Trouble arises when we put everything upside down. Nature sets up things in such a way that women get pregnant. They must not go hunting in that condition. Today, we tell our daughters they can be pregnant and run after a deer. I have seen a woman with a big belly toiling eight hours a day for five days a week in a warehouse. When she returns home to her natural habitat, she cooks dinner and cares for the kids. Modern society has made it more difficult for women. We must organize society and improve things in such a way that the work of the man may be sufficient to provide for the family. It has always been that way since dawn.

I am not advocating sending women back to the kitchen; I am calling for an equity-based program where those women who want to operate in their natural habitats have their contributions considered and their needs met. Not all women have masculine features; some women are born feminine and would like to thrive in their universe and have their contributions recognized. Some women don't want to reproduce; they want to preserve their bodies and operate like men; society must also allow them to live as they please. We must not put everybody in the same basket because, right now, we put together masculine and feminine women in the same club and treat them regardless of reality. A woman who chooses celibacy cannot be compared with the one who desires to be in a relationship. Some who choose to swim in the partnership pool want to reproduce and enjoy their natural right, while others prefer to preserve their bodies. Society needs to consider the imbroglio and address it.

If we don't know how to set up the problem of feminism, we will lay more burden upon the shoulders of our daughters. No one can be pregnant and toil in warehouses; it is unacceptable. Unfortunately, we teach our daughters they can, and they are doing it. Can we hold man responsible for such a burden upon our daughters?

Man and woman are different. In contrast, anatomy and morphology distinguish males from females, while physiology and psychology separate men from women. The anatomy unites them to become one flesh; psychology makes them a winning team. The scriptures summarize the situation in Ecclesiastes 4: 10-12 as follows:

"Two are better than one, because they have a good return for their labor: If either of them falls down, one can help the other up. But pity anyone who falls and has no one to help them up. Also, if two lie down together, they will keep warm. But how can one keep warm alone? Though one may be overpowered, two can defend themselves. A cord of three strands is not quickly broken."

It is not sexism but reality, which we tend to forget between men and women. In the introduction of her book "A Vindication of the Rights of Women," Mary Wollstonecraft, the mother of the feminist movement, noticed this statement to be the law of nature. She said the physical difference between men and women could not be denied; in her own words, I quote:

"It is observable that the female is, so far as strength is concerned, inferior to the male."

Man and woman are indissociable; they are inseparable because they are riveted together. We make a huge mistake when we talk about independence between these two entities; they are one. None plays a greater role; they complete and complement each other. We need a rotor and a stator to produce electricity; no part is more important than the other. Without one, the other is useless; both must necessarily be together to be defined.

Materialist scientists often believe the difference between man and woman might come from the brain, but things are not obvious. The male and female brains are almost identical, and no one can easily differentiate by simple observation alone. The male brain is slightly bigger because female humans are less robust than males. However, their minds are totally different. Men don't have the same Will and Representation as women.

As we already defined it, the mind is the electromagnetic activity that hovers over the brain. The mind creates our reality, and it does so when consciousness is projected on the screen of the mind. The fluctuation of the mind creates a particular phenomenon known as depression. Today, we know depression has its root cause in the cardiovascular system. Everything starts with a perturbation that roils through the cardiovascular system, causing two known conditions: hypotension and hypertension. These two states cause poor brain perfusion, sending the mind into depression.

The statistics show that women are more prone to depression and anxiety than men. The incidence rate of Alzheimer's disease[20] is also higher in women than men; they are also more likely to develop dementia than men. This phenomenon depends on the physiology of men and women.

Today, biology offers us enormous clues, and we know how cells function in the body. Men and women might carry the same Information, but their activation makes the difference. Both baby boys and girls develop out of one single fetus; the embryo has no gender identity until sex organs begin to differentiate a few weeks after fertilization. Gene expressions control all the processes. This shows that boys and girls have identical Information in their bodies, but some critical information becomes dormant while some are activated. The difference between man and woman depends on the manifestation of genes both individuals carry in their chromosomes; our daughters must be aware of the science behind the phenomenon.

Radical feminists are looking for someone to blame. Thus, to reach their goal, they manipulate our daughters. What men have done against women was wrong, but it is not a reason to foment a coup to destabilize our society.

---

[20] This brief report shows Alzheimer's is greater in women than men; Beam, C., Kaneshiro, C., Jang, J., Reynolds, C., Pedersen, N., and Gatz, M. (2018) "Differences Between Women and Men in Incidence Rates of Dementia and Alzheimer's Disease," Journal of Alzheimer's Disease

Life is still a mystery, and there are many things we don't understand. If we go against reality, our society will be destroyed. Unfortunately, we seem to be engaged on that pathway rather than amending our society. People often say one of the signs of intelligence is to accept the facts without being offended.

A recent study tackles a controversial topic of human intelligence; the researchers expect to elucidate why men tend to overestimate their intelligence, but do men really overestimate themselves? I do not want our daughters to remain ignorant on this subject; the more we know about man and woman constitution, the better our society will be. Some topics are irrelevant, but people keep venturing into that field because many still don't understand life and its manifestation. Too many people don't know life is doing its own things; it is the same life that branches out as man and woman.

Any topic related to intelligence makes waves because of the concept of the white man. Modern society is stained forever with European thinkers and achievers who used racial connotations to dominate the rest of the world. Through social Darwinism and Eugenics, they spread false teachings, but today, the Japanese and Koreans are proof the concept of the white man is a sheer fallacy. Although the hue of their skin is almost the same as that of the Europeans, these people were labeled yellow. Some Koreans are even brighter in complexion than the Spaniards and Portuguese. Tell me that the white man is rich, powerful, beautiful, and talented, and I would agree without a whimper. But the white man is white and often gets stuck in my throat. On balance, I finally understand our society since anyone can choose to be a woman; the white has set the rhythm. A man with fair skin, a black beard and hair, who believes he is white does not want to accept an individual who undergoes hormonal therapy to call herself a woman. In a society where we have rejected science, if we ask what a woman is, we must also ask what a white man is. Jesus requests we get the beam out of our own eyes before taking the mote from our neighbor's eyes. The white man is in his fantasy; he must not forbid other people to fancy their universe as they please. A famous television host said everyone has his own truth.

We need science to put some order in our society. With science, we know all these doctrines are false, yet we still maintain them and teach them in school to our kids. We don't assign sex to the newborn; we observe the genitalia of the infant and acknowledge it. Nobody hates the white man and conspires to wipe his race out of this planet; These are all fallacies. The white man is the superior race, therefore, the most intelligent. An individual is not intelligent because he has less melanin in his skin. Here comes the question: what is intelligence?

We cannot define intelligence without looking closely at the human mind. The human mind could be divided into two sections: the seminal mind and the creative mind. Both sections comprise three frequencies. The seminal mind has wakefulness, awareness, and alertness, and the creative mind is made of imagination, intuition, and dreaming. Let's note in passing that humans grow with their minds. The infant is born with wakefulness, then he acquires awareness and later alertness. One of the sub-frequencies of awareness is self-awareness, and science does not know when it arises in the child's mind.

Human intelligence could be defined as the ability to use the creative mind to efficiently solve quotidian problems the individual is confronted with in his life. That said, intelligence has its external components because it depends on a feedback loop mechanism. The more the individual has challenges, the more likely he will develop his mind to adapt. Life is still a mystery, and several other parameters may be involved in the process. Still, we know physiology and psychology play a key role in forming the individual's thinking ability. There is no intelligence without critical thinking, and on that, men are better equipped than women, and we will demonstrate it shortly.

As we know, life on planet Earth is exclusively challenging; we live to solve problems. After solving a problem, the individual becomes happy and moves forward, awaiting another problem. All humans and almost all living creatures live the same way, continually fighting elements to preserve life in their bodies. Therefore, the Austrian physicist Erwin Schrodinger saw life as a struggle against entropy.

If existence is about solving problems, there is no doubt that men are equipped to be more intelligent than women in the universe of transcendence, but women will be better off in immanence. As history shows, men tend to occupy space and face more challenges that allow them to develop certain traits over time. If women are confronted with the same problem, they will yield the same capacity and ability over time. If so, the situation in comparing men's and women's intelligence becomes irrelevant. Science says all human species roaming the Earth originate from Africa, meaning both came from the same source. A colony of ants operates on a function-based scale. The queen lays eggs, the soldiers defend the colony, and workers perform various tasks to keep the settlement thriving. Could we compare the queen with a soldier ant?

There is no way to compare men and women; we are in grave error whenever we start comparing men and women. Both are condemned to be in an obligatory symbiotic relationship. Man gets nothing without a woman, and woman, in return, has nothing without a man. These types of studies gaslight human society and tend to destabilize the community. Why do we continue throwing the taxpayers' money through the window with futile studies while real challenges stand before us? Notice that Europe and its patriarchal system originate all these troubles. I understand and cannot disagree with you when you said that women's dependence served men's economic interests; the European man has always labored in that direction, always working in the dark to sap women's mentality and destroy their self-esteem. That's how he succeeds in sitting his hegemony; his mind is continually busy with projects of domination and conquest. Although all lands have been conquered and occupied, the white man continues squirming and jiggling for adventures. He must create commotion and unrest in human gatherings because he cannot really appreciate peace. It's genetic; Charlemagne also never rested; he was continually at war. Amid chaos and trouble, the white man finds a purpose, which he never knows.

My point here is to denounce any study that tends to pull men and women apart. While former scientific studies toiled to demean women, current investigations tend to demote men. There is no way to envision men and women separately;

they are realities of the same coin. We cannot oppose them because they are not opposite; we cannot compare them because they are incomparable. Nothing describes them better than a rotor and stator working together to produce electricity to illuminate the city; independently, they are useless parts, ready to be thrown away.

Physiology and psychology define man and woman. Each individual is designed to play a specific role in society. Materialist scientists bring division when they believe human life springs from a random event, thus assigning no purpose and meaning to life, but the fact is in front of us. Life has a purpose, and there is a meaning to life. There is functional Information behind the life of all living organisms on Earth. Evolution was not a random act but a directed process. Man and woman are designed to occupy specific posts in the formation of life; thus, they were designed so. As we can notice, with lion pride, the females go hunting while the males defend the territory. Roles are shared to preserve harmony within the community of lions, and there is no other way around it. Nobody complains because the male lions don't carry stupid scientific studies to demote and demean the female lions. Even animals know that cooperation is vital for their survival. Male lions don't make a fool of their females until they desire to grow a mane and balls. Only male humans continually harass their females and push them to question their value. God also gives women patience so they don't pour water into their nostrils while they are still babies. Women's compassion and love are so great that they keep nurturing their boys, knowing they will grow up to demean them. There is nothing more ridiculous than calling what gives you life inferior. Women cultivate babies from their own resources; they fabricate the male piece by piece through a forty-week-long and tedious gestation period. Seeing the current affairs of the world, if women drowned their baby boys, they would be justified, but they choose not to because forgiveness is godlier than punishment, and compassion is more powerful than anger.

The study says men overestimate their intelligence, but they don't, and the facts are outside there to prove it. This type of study must not even be a subject of debate because it is irrelevant; there is no need to avenge women by vilifying men either. From antiquity to the scientific revolution, men have proved their points throughout history. Do they overestimate their potential? The evidence says no! The Information men carry in their DNA allows them to do such prowess, and there is nothing they have to brag about; women would do the same things if they carried these specific genes. Life unfolds according to sets of data we hold in our chromosomes, and these codons are not arranged randomly.

When invaders stormed the village to kill and loot, it was not the moment to doubt oneself. Men are equipped with these special genes that spring into action, pumping adrenaline and cortisol into their systems, and they become angry enough to deal with the invaders. While men are fighting, the Information inside women allows them to find shelter for the progeny. They are more efficient in that task than men; it is teamwork, and each has to be efficient in his function. If we ever switch roles, it will be a disaster. Men will not perform the job that requires immanence qualities better than women, and women will not be more efficient in defending the village than men could have done it. We are wrong when we start comparing man and woman; it is a sacrilege we must stop doing. We go against nature when we turn our daughters against our sons. Women thrive by immanence, and they could never kill the enemies and protect the village better than men could have done it. Everything is in the right place until we begin to compare. There is trouble in our society when radical feminists, triggered by mediocre men, want to defy the natural order of things. Men are equipped to have self-esteem in their field, which is transcendence. When it comes to playing in the field of immanence, I bet women would be better than men. They would feel more natural and have self-esteem than a man could feel.

A man will be more confident going to war than a woman; it is a fact. During the war in Ukraine, women did not tell men to run to safety; I saw the opposite. We must stop gaslighting our community by opposing our daughters to our sons, our sisters to our brothers. They are called to become one flesh, and they are inseparable; therefore, indissociable.

This particular topic also answers the question people often ask when it comes to engineering class or the study of mathematics or physics. People usually ask why there are few women in these classes. People should stop asking these irrelevant questions because life is not a competition. Failure to understand life and its manifestation leads people to ask such questions. Why do people want women to study engineering to operate as construction workers or structural engineers when they are unhappy doing that job? Since when do humans pick up jobs to respond to competition? What is the meaning of existence?

Women don't venture into certain fields of study because the Information inside their bodies does not allow them to thrive in the universe of transcendence. Mathematics, physics, and engineering require men to deploy particular Information that does not make women comfortable; it's simple. Their body systems are not equipped to process these types of Information in the same way men's systems cannot treat pregnancy-related Information. We are in trouble because science is late to understand this phenomenon; life always unfolds based on the functional Information we carry in our chromosomes. Humans are not the author of life, and no matter how we lie to ourselves and our children, reality stands in front of us. We have just buried our heads like an ostrich, not to see the fact. Some areas of study lead to specific occupations, and women don't blossom over there. It does not mean women cannot do it because you will find some doing it. We must not forget that reincarnation exists, and certain women are born loaded and equipped to excel in jobs that require transcendence.

Women are not comfortable fighting in a battle where humans butcher other human beings because they are designed to carry life. Women are the guardians of life; remember that they fabricate babies out of scratch, which is quite impressive. Women are not comfortable making war; however, you can find some that do well in the killing, but her dominant Information is not destruction but creation. A woman is programmed to give birth; she stands with life and must not participate in the agenda of death. It is mediocre men who tell women that they can also kill as men do. Killing is not a thing one should be proud of; mediocre men glorify it. Social Darwinism makes the subject a hot topic to discuss, but the observation speaks for itself.

I have remarked that a pride of lions barely overcome a single crocodile and one-on-one, there is no match; a lion cannot win. However, a jaguar or a leopard easily wins the same battle. A jaguar has the necessary information in his DNA to overpower a caiman, but notice how a lion always wins over a leopard. Someone may oppose and cry out, but yes, there are animals a lion cannot stand in the jungle. Life unfolds based on functional Information in our DNA. Most animals live by instinct, but humans, in addition to their instinct, have a quest for knowledge. People often argue that culture establishes gender roles, but this is not true because humans also live by instinct. Two voluminous breasts and menstrual cramps in a few days and every month don't make women the best soldiers to defend the city. Through pregnancy, women internalize their entropy; they incubate over it and convert it into useful energy to fabricate a baby. Men externalize chaos in their body systems to perform heavy-duty work and fight battles. Disorder always wants to pull things apart; women are designed to take advantage of it through immanence, while men are programmed to use it through transcendence.

Women are programmed differently. In sports, for instance, rarely will you find a woman win in men's competitions, but a man will usually win in women's competitions. It is a fact that is undeniable. It is scientific because we can test it and reproduce it everywhere on this planet and get the same result. A professional soccer group made of women will not beat a team composed of men. The same rule applies in almost all disciplines of the sport. Why is it so? Morphology and anatomy define males and females. And we know men thrive by transcendence, and women reign over a universe of immanence. This statement is testable scientifically; there is no argument against it.

Even in sexuality, women prefer active men who dominate in bed to men who are clumsy in their movement and passive. In my personal observation and experiment, I have noticed that women are not comfortable playing the role of transcendence in bed, even given the opportunity. Very few women will take action in bed, but sexuality is not about proving a point; it is about enjoying the act. Women are at the receiving end, and they enjoy the act when it is properly given. The scriptures recommend men love their wives, not the opposite. The rotor is called to take action to produce electricity. Life becomes exciting when we follow and yield to the program governing the body. The world is in chaos when we rebel. I do not attribute the trouble in the world to women, though; men are responsible, continually harassing women with irrelevant topics: why aren't women in mathematics or engineering classes? Why do they want them to be?

Women can, but they are not naturally designed for it, so why waste time and do whatever one cannot enjoy? Saying the opposite is a lie we keep telling our children. Life is about blossoming; we thrive on bearing fruit and enjoying it. Life is about happiness, and only people who deny it harass women with such topics. Why push women to do things they are uncomfortable with? What is the purpose? Today, we have forced women to the brim until they start revolting. Some want to hang out separately. But the truth is, even in their intimacy, female to female, they often buy an artificial genitalia that is shaped like a phallus. Why? If we shut down our manufactured ideologies and doctrines, our world will be better off. What if the non-flesh entity pilots the body as he pleases? In this life, he rolls in a male body, and the next, he chooses to ride a female. We still don't know; for that cause, we must be careful. Life is more complex than we may think, but existence is simple.

However, we know that the females are designed as receptacles to receive the action and the seed. The stator cannot play the role of the rotor; they cannot operate independently either; both need each other. Nothing is random as they pretend and want us to believe; everything is designed with a purpose, working to help life multiply and break away and scatter throughout the universe. Elon Musk, Jeff Bezos, and Nasa scientists are working on it already; we must admit the point of entry proposal[21] is correct until we find alien life outside. The existence of aliens does not cancel God's presence because recent physics research proves mass is not a fundamental property, positing the existence of an unknown realm.

While the female and male brains may look similar, men's and women's minds are entirely different. The intellectual quotient of men and women may not differ either, but how both individuals express their intelligence is completely different. Men manifest their intelligence better in the field involved in transcendence, while women thrive in the field of immanence. Both sexes are equally intelligent and become a phenomenon when they join forces; that's why they produce a baby when they are united in intimacy. If we don't accept life as it is, we will run aground. Life is still a mystery; the best thing to do is stop asking

---

[21] The point of entry proposal is a corollary of the no-boundary proposal of Stephen Hawking, which posits that life has a single-entry point into the material universe. The reader can learn more by reading the following paper: Zanou, D. (2021) "The Point of Entry Proposal" Amazon KDP

irrelevant questions. A woman can fabricate a human being out of thin air; that alone surpasses all engineering. Who among men can do that? Since no man can accomplish such prowess, men denigrate the act and reduce it to something insignificant. Mediocre men are continually after women to sap their mentality because they cannot understand both individuals are inseparable and indissociable. Dear ma'am, do you know any polite way to tell humans that man and woman are incomparable? I tried as hard as I could; reality is an undeniable fact. There is no other way to prove evidence than observation. Life becomes unbearable because humans have locked themselves in a false narrative.

If I say I love you, I mean it because I have come to agree with you that men have created the trouble we have in this world; not all men, but the ones you call "mediocre men." Mediocre men have destroyed our world because they feel insecure and shoulder the responsibility upon women. To feel important in their own eyes, they have to compare themselves with women; Einstein did not compare himself with any woman. Olympe de Gouges called all women to wake up; she was right because women have been so naïve to believe men's lies. Some of them still feel guilty for what Eve did in the Garden of Eden. It was not Eve's fault but Adam's because God gave the order to Adam, who was supposed to instruct his wife; he failed to convey the message correctly and blamed his wife. Mediocre men always blame women.

There is another particular group of men I don't want our daughters to ignore. I have already talked about them but briefly; now, I want to delve into the topic and dissect it. These men are of class three, and I call them high entropy men. These men are particular in that they have more extra energy, and some of them succeed in finding a way to channel that energy for the good of the community. If these people fail to manage the chaos of their bodies, society often gets into trouble; they also have a specific behavior.

First, I have to inform our daughters that low entropy women cannot marry them because they are incompatible. A woman of class one cannot marry a man of class three; this type of union does not last; sooner or later, the couple will split apart because women of class one have acts of service as love language while these men are into physical contact. They continually long for sex; therefore, they are in the opposition phase with class one women.

Society does not understand these men and often crushes them. In general rule, women are behind the success of these men, but unfortunately, their fall is also due to women. Women build them, and women also destroy them. There is nothing wrong with high entropy men; they are regular people who have extra energy than ordinary fellows. How can an individual know he or she is of high entropy?

The individual is often agitated and has difficulty focusing. His attention is broken every second, and his mind is inundated with sexual imagery and desires. For that cause, high entropy men often struggle with academic studies. I recommend they not go to university because they will waste money and time. They have extra energy to do more than others; they can go the extra mile, offering them a tremendous advantage in terms of work. As Elon Musk said, nobody changes the world by working forty hours a week, and high entropy people are equipped to double this amount. However, they need to understand the society we have built and find the right field of operation. One of their challenges is to find the best way to vent their extra energy. Some find an evacuation canal through work, others through sex, but the worst is through crime.

High entropy people crave risks; consequently, any job that requires adrenaline flushing the body systems is their field of preference. They thrive well in the Army, police force, fire rescue division, and related field jobs where people manage space. They don't work in offices unless the job requires adrenaline gushing into their body systems. If nothing occupies them in office jobs, they will create trouble for women around, and most of the time, they pile up cases of sexual assaults. They are like a rooster in the henhouse.

These individuals can be brokers or investors, and because their sense of risk is high, they often tend to engage in fraudulent activities. It takes an increased sense of control and a strong woman to keep high-entropy men on the right path. They have reckless behavior and estimate danger poorly. Their imagination flourishes well because their minds are continually busy.

High-entropy men's life is full of ups and downs; their existence is often caught up between sex, money, and power. Adult life is hinged on work, represented here as money, and relationships that stand as sex. Since these individuals are never satisfied with these two pillars, they are often in trouble; that's why they cannot marry anyhow. They need strong women who can understand them, and low entropy women are excluded. However, if our daughters fall in love with one, they must realize there is extra energy pushing their husbands; for that cause, they must toil to assist the man in coping with it. One example of a high entropy guy in the Bible is King David; another is Samson. Great power comes with great responsibility, and trouble does not stand far away.

If a class-three man fails to manage his entropy, he will end up in jail; it is an inevitable passage for high-entropy people who fail to cope with the phenomenon. The majority of the carceral population is composed of high entropy guys; they fail to control the fire within. The gift turns into a curse, the extra energy they possess has destroyed them. Parents must understand the phenomenon to assist their teenagers. Cigarettes, alcohol, weeds, and narcotic drugs are early signs of the manifestation of a high entropy in the body systems.

Sexuality is the best outlet to vent the extra energy; the second option is working and making money, which is a good option since we live in a capitalistic society. Sex and money are intertwined in high entropy people's lives; they must find the sweet spot. Unfortunately, many fail because people have no cognizance of this phenomenon, and our society is intolerant. Our communities don't understand these individuals and often label them devils. They don't have demons; they are normal individuals that function differently. They must be aware of jobs they cannot do and places they cannot go because of their chaotic Representation; they see chaos. These people cannot be clergymen; otherwise, nuns will suffer in the convent.

Changes in classes of entropy naturally occur as individuals grow up; as we know, girls upgrade, and boys downgrade; the middle class is the most stable, and most adult humans in marital relationships live there. The individual can shift his class by increasing or decreasing his testosterone level; it can be done naturally through physical and mental exercise, diet, and talking techniques; hormone therapy is another option. I personally test this phenomenon (naturally, I chose to be a clergyman from the beginning), and I can testify that low entropy people are not condemned to binge on food, and high entropy guys are not locked up in drugs and criminality; one can walk out of his class of entropy as he decides. The individual controls many aspects of his life; entropy does not take charge of our lives unless we allow it. However, it is easier to upgrade than downgrade. This means parents with high entropy teens have more work to do; if they spot the phenomenon early, they can anticipate it and assist the kid genuinely. It is not a hopeless case, but the population's ignorance makes it a tragedy. Those who are aware will direct and guide their kids accordingly.

There is one crucial piece of information our daughters must never forget about high entropy men: never get pregnant without their consent. Like the narcissist woman you describe in chapter 11 of the second volume, High entropy men are self-absorbed individuals who pass their needs before anyone else. In no circumstance shall our daughters carry a child for these men unless they ask for a baby. If ladies scoff at this simple advice, they will pay it dearly for the rest of their lives. High entropy people are ready to settle if their thirst for sex, money, and power is quenched. These individuals are parched and continually crave sex, adventure, and money unless they are spiritual and succeed in finding equilibrium. A child must be a business of two individuals; a woman cannot decide independently. Often, women make this error, thinking they will conquer the man if they get pregnant. Men don't have the same Representation as women; this is a fact.

Women often believe men think like them; a man is not a woman, and vice versa; their minds are different. It is natural for women to believe that a man will love them more if they get pregnant because a baby brings joy to a mother. In this modern society, a baby consumes time and money, and men don't want to sacrifice these two assets unless they are ready to settle. Women don't understand this equation, and many fall into the trap and end up alone. Most single mothers could have avoided much burden if they understood the constitution of a man. Man thrives by transcendence, and most men usually settle as their appetite for sex, money, and sometimes power is appeased; that's why young girls are called to seek mature men when they want to build a family. A man who has spent time working for a while and saved money is a good candidate. Notice that high entropy people often downgrade as they get into relationships. Your compatriot Nadine has a pertinent take on the question. In her interview with Thierry Ardisson, during the promotion of one of her books, she said, "if people pay a little bit of attention before getting married, there will not be all the drama we have nowadays." I stand with her; things are not working between man and woman because society lacks knowledge about human existence on planet Earth.

A young girl who starts adulthood at twenty-one can look up to a man of twenty-seven and up; we live in a modern society, and marriage is not a joke. The youth often don't know why they get together, and women still don't grasp the reality of existence. Boys don't start adulthood desiring to have kids; it is rare to find a boy craving to have a baby in his early twenties; girls have such desire. That's why girls who want to settle must look up, not down. Some women run after men younger than them because radical feminism teaches women to do as they please; as a result, they increase women's burden. There is nothing wrong with it if the young man can provide because marriage is not about luxury but responsibility. Age is indeed a number. Still, women must understand the underlying mechanism of man's constitution and the limitations Nature imposes on women. Man and woman are not operating under the same clock.

Moreover, we don't marry to change people, and men naturally crave sex and adventure unless the individual is of low entropy. Radical feminists have toiled in the last century to prove that man is like woman and today, we have the result: broken families and single mothers in our communities. The truth hurts, but it will become part of their systems if women accept and digest it. Life is not a tragedy, and our daughters must not live to make it one. If they heed the functional Information embedded in their bodies, they will avoid unnecessary trouble; forewarned is forearmed! Humans are suffering because they live by ideologies and doctrines instead of reality.

Radical feminists and materialist scientists worked to promote an agenda; they shoveled their doctrines into our throats without considering the reality. They have laid more burden upon women because they told our sisters that men are like them; they are not. Rape in marital relationships is one reason I open up about this reality. It is not acceptable that our daughters marry to suffer in the relationship; I will come back to this particular topic later. As I have said, men are not monsters; women don't understand them. Men also, in return, have no cognizance of the constitution of a woman. That's why some men flirt with hotel maids; they think women also go gallivanting around the city. Women long for intimacy; they don't crave sex as men do. Hollywood teaches our children that a woman can go down the street and pick up a man to have one night. I am not saying it is impossible because some women are on hormones, and some are of high entropy, but these are rare cases. Women naturally don't function that way; their biology does not operate that way. Wollstonecraft wanted women to become more masculine to be worthy of respect. I urge our daughters to be more feminine to thrive in their universe. Life is not a competition, and we request an equity-based program instead of an equality-based agenda.

Humans are conscious agents, and life moves us in a certain way. We are medium consciousness, meaning we have one particular frequency called personhood. Professor Michio Kaku defines consciousness as a feedback loop mechanism, the entity process to reach a goal in the future. He means humans manage space and compute time; for that cause, the future is significant for us because goals are always in the future. And evolution equips us with something called hope to deal with the situation; here is another subject I do not want our daughters to neglect. They must not remain in the dark about it.

Hope is critical to human life; it is a topic that concerns more boys than girls. However, it is recommended our daughters know about it to help their sons navigate the meanders of life. As I have always said, morphology and anatomy differentiate males from females, but physiology and psychology define man and woman. A man is not a woman and vice versa; they have a different psychology. The statistics show males commit suicide at thrice the rate of females[22]. There is no surprise in this fact because, as you said, Nature designs men to thrive by transcendence and women by immanence. Challenges build the man, but he is crushed whenever he finds no way out of the trouble.

Conscientious people often say teen suicide is one of the things that scare them the most as parents. And I respond, you don't need to worry because the scriptures already answer the question: hope. Suicide occurs when there is no hope, and whenever the individual falls into a bottomless pit, the idea of suicide haunts the mind. For this cause, I would like to instruct the youth and parents about hope. Most of the time, hope and faith work hand in hand. Hope is a life force; it is the aspiration for something to materialize in the future. On the other hand, as defined in the scriptures, faith is the assurance of things hoped for, the evidence of things not seen with our physical eyes. Faith connects the individual with hope.

Let me use the analogy of the fisherman to clarify it. A fisherman throws his pole into a river, and a fish takes the bait. Here, the fish is the hope, and the line that connects the fish to the rod in the hand of the fisherman is faith. While the fish is still underwater and not seen, the fisherman has a conviction of something on the hook and starts pulling the line to him.

---

[22] Here is a short article that displays the statistics of suicide in Canada; Nabaneelan, T. (2012) "Suicide rates: An overview" suicideinfo.ca

Hope is important for humans to keep going in life; it is vital for survival. People often die when there is nothing on the hook; if the individual expects nothing in the future, death seems to be preferable. Nobody commits suicide while having hope; it is like someone who goes to the restaurant, orders a meal, pays for everything, and leaves without being served. Hope is more important than faith, although faith is the engine that brings what is hoped for to the individual. We cling unto life as long as we have hope. Jeremiah 29:11 said the following:

"For I know the thoughts that I think toward you, saith the Lord, thoughts of peace, and not of evil, to give you an expected end."

When there is no vision, the people perish, said King Solomon. Today, in this modern society, the youth and parents need to understand this phenomenon that causes suicide; one variation of the phenomenon is mass shootings. And both suicide and mass shootings involve more men than women. Our daughters need to understand the phenomenon to train their boys. Suicide and mass shootings have almost the same root: lack of hope. With suicide, the individual does not designate a culprit for his suffering. Even if he identifies or thinks there is a malefactor, he has no means to avenge himself or chooses not to move through that pathway.

In contrast, mass shootings point the finger at a malefactor. The individual devises a plan and convinces himself in his mind that the designated culprit must pay for his crime. Terrorism falls into this pathway, and the whole process moves as follows: conception-justification-action.

Sometimes, the conception is founded; there are many cases where it has no foundation; the individual makes up things based on assumptions and fake news or his flourishing imagination. The Charlie Hebdo shooting is one absurdity.

And just yesterday, a gunman opened fire at a supermarket in one neighborhood of Buffalo, a city in New York. He brutally murdered ten people and injured three in the name of the Great Replacement conspiracy theory; that's what happens when people lose track of reality. When the youth cannot see the end of the tunnel because society feeds them lies, life becomes a tragedy. When we don't know anymore that the Native Indians were here on this land before we came in, trouble may arise. When we forget that these black people had their ancestors enslaved and forced out of Africa against their own volition, we may nourish the desire to exterminate them.

A week later, another 18-year-old boy reiterated the macabre performance in Texas and waltzed into an elementary school to fatally shoot nineteen students and two teachers. The United States is at war against itself; we watch our children butchered in front of us and helplessly shed tears. We see no purpose in life and attribute no meaning to existence. Our children grow up without any landmarks.

A tragedy like this often strikes when parents fail in their jobs. Life is a childhood preparation, and the scriptures explicitly explained in Proverb 22: 6, I quote:

"Train up a child in the way he should go, and when he is old, he will not depart from it."

Nowadays, too many parents seem not to be prepared for the job. Some are not aware of the society we have built; the Western society is a capitalistic society with a patriarchal denomination. This means the man leads the house and puts food on the table. Too many people seem to forget this reality, and the result is what we see: children grow up anxious and confused. The man is nothing but a boy when the training session is botched. Age is just a number; some individuals start making money at a very young age, while some at fifty are still struggling to make ends meet.

When men lack vision in life, they are up to committing absurdity, and sometimes they end up with atrocities. Our boys must not lack hope because it is a life force that propels the individual every day. One must get up from bed expecting this day to be better than yesterday and tomorrow to be even brighter. If this motivation is lacking in our lives, the mind will fall into the bottomless pit. And the individual will either commit suicide or kill other people to avenge his parents' failure. To avoid one of these scenarios, our youngsters must be equipped with hope; the youth will perish without hope, and boys need it more than girls.

A man cannot live without hope because he is naturally designed as the pilot of the house; a pilot must always have a roadmap. Women are the guardians of life; they are designed to assist the pilot. However, as our society has evolved, women could also be pilots. Women don't commit suicide often because they have a natural challenge: their kids' education. They often see their kids as a seed they plant. Anyone who puts grain in the ground always waits to see it sprout and grow. We can also say that women are more patient than men. They have a natural predisposition because of their ability to carry a pregnancy to term; having a womb causes women to be continually flushed with particular hormones that soothe their personality. Boys or girls, anyone who has hope could boldly state as David did in Psalm 16:6, I quote:

"The lines have fallen to me in pleasant places; yea, I have a goodly heritage."

To sum up, man and woman are two incomparable entities, similar to a rotor and its stator. A man is a person who dominates the male body, while a woman is a person who reigns in the female body. One must be woman in her personality before ruling a female body to be a woman; that means biology alone does not define a woman. A person is a non-flesh entity, a spiritual being with no gender identity but only expresses itself within a physical body as a man or a woman. Anatomy and morphology separate the male from the female, while physiology and psychology help differentiate the man from the woman. The male body is strongly built and bigger in size compared to the female[23]. The man piloting the male body is unstable because of a high level of testosterone flushing the body systems. The woman is relatively more stable because of oxytocin, putting women in class one while men occupy class three. Men have high entropy; as a result, they have chaotic Representation as consciousness is projected on the screen of their minds.

---

[23] This type of assertions fall into the domain of social science, which always deals with aggregate data. There are females who are bigger than male humans, but here we speak based on the general rule. The same remark applies to entropy classification. The reader need to pay attention and understand what is social science to avoid any amalgam.

Women have a beautiful Representation, perceiving a world of harmony and love. Men and women are essentially the same; they differ by function. Their existence brings the differentiation, and they don't see the same reality; we conclude a man is not a woman and vice versa. Any woman who grasps this reality has a tremendous advantage when searching for a life partner to build a family.

Third Distinction:
Dating and Marriage

Now that we know life is exclusively challenging and men don't have the same Representation of the world as women do, our daughters need to wake up to reality. They need to realize that existence is no longer displayed in the village. For that cause, the individual must necessarily get her self-awareness operation done before entering adulthood. The girl must clearly define who she is, what she wants, and where she is going through that operation. She must choose one pool between celibacy and partnership. She must also decide if she wants to build a family and raise children. These are the two fundamental choices our daughters must make during the self-awareness operation that occurs mostly around seventeen or eighteen. They must establish themselves before leaving high school.

Our daughters must set themselves up because time is ticking against them, and there is nothing we can do against it; life is not fair, and we must learn to deal with it. The next step is to understand a marital relationship and distinguish it from dating. Marriage is a concession and granting of rights; it's two stories clashing in a tiny portion of land called a house. The fundamental goal here is to create a family to have a home.

In a marital relationship, we accord some rights to our partner to dispose of, possess, and care for our body. The only way we succeed in this endeavor is through unconditional love, which technically does not exist or is not within reach of humans. We only tend toward it; the closer we get, the better.

Love is what is needed in a marital relationship, not self-love. Love gives, forgives, and serves; self-love takes, uses, and forgets. I would like to delve into this concept because people often confound love with self-love and attachment; they are not the same thing.

Frankly speaking, love is only applied to conscious agents; we could spread that application throughout the animal and plant kingdom, but love cannot be applied to inanimate objects. Unfortunately, we love things; we are supposed to like objects and love living organisms. Even such application is sometimes problematic because we often hear people say, "I love fish." And a Rabbi questions them, why do you take it from the water and boil it? The individual pretends to love fish, yet he takes it from the river, cooks it, and eats it. Humans are appalling; usually, they fail to listen to themselves when they speak. People use the verb "love" without really understanding its meaning. Plato described love in the Symposium as the everlasting possession of the good. Today, with science, we know that love is the highest vibration of the human heart. We focus on the heart because it is the most important organ in the body, and death always emanates from it. Remember that the spirit sets its command post over there. Whatever affects the heart will affect the body and threaten the individual's life.

Love is the fundamental attribute of the creative energy that emanates from the immaterial realm. Pure consciousness is love and is the concatenation of Information and Order.

We recognize love through its fundamental properties: giving, forgiveness, and service. The corruption of love due to the presence of entropy in the material universe generates human love and self-love, which are set respectively at 10% and 0% of the scale if we put unconditional love at 100%.

Humans are called to grow love from the 10% upward, and we give tithe thereon. We measure the degree of the individual's love when she moves from 10% upward, and her love expression is in bad shape when it tends toward 0%. Nobody living in the flesh can pretend to reach 100%; we only grow closer to that value.

While self-love is dangerous in the marital relationship, it is a valuable tool in business. Our daughters need self-interest and self-love to succeed in business in this modern society. We recommend dropping self-love at the sill of the door when coming home and taking it back when returning to work. It is always about love and attachment between a husband and a wife, never self-love. Attachment occurs when we gain certainty about the sentiment of our partner, and then we commit to living together. It happens at the fifth rung of our ladder of love; we devise seven steps to follow for our daughters to have a healthy relationship. Attachment is only between partners and not children. Unfortunately, humans get attached to their children and the material things, hence the source of much of their suffering. It hurts when we lose something we like and someone we love. Since nobody will get out of this material world alive, we should reduce our attachment to only one individual we share the journey with; that individual is our running mate. We are called to be attached to our life partner; we must be one flesh in marriage. Unfortunately, people don't understand that and get hooked on other people as well; some avoid their running partners to bond with their children or siblings.

Wives are not supposed to get attached to their children, and they eventually end up doing so because their partners are often abusive. And to find refuge, women go after their children to make an unhealthy bond with them(this is not about sex). Women suffer in relationships; for that cause, they must be aware of the seven steps that compose a healthy relationship to navigate the process efficiently. Adult life is hinged on work and relationships; women's biology urges them to focus most of their energy on relationships. A woman is likely to enjoy life more if she hits the jackpot with her relationship. We do not know why, but that's how things are so designed; women measure their success by the state of their love affair. Men weigh their success by their work and bank account; that's a reality we often mock, but we cannot scoff at Nature. Our society is upside down because we scoff at this phenomenon that governs our biology. We can find some clues in the Bible, and the reality also corroborates the assertion. Women don't necessarily need money to be happy; a lovely partner full of attention and affection is always preferred. The following verse in Proverbs 15: 17 explains it well:

"Better is a dinner of herbs where love is, than a stalled ox and hatred therewith."

Love is what defines a woman, so a relationship is always their priority, unbeknownst to the individual. Women reign over a universe of immanence; those aware of this fact manage the journey accordingly and make it happily and successfully. Most women don't know what to look for when boys approach them; on the flip side, boys always know what they look for in girls. I know it will not surprise you; most men and boys seek what women have between their legs. This harsh reality must sink deep into our daughters' ears. Most men are into sex, and physical appearance is what counts for them. Unfortunately, being a beautiful woman does not mean she craves sex; that's one of the reasons many relationships flop. To help our daughters navigate the process and avoid the trap of men gallivanting around the city, we build a ladder of love that comprises seven steps. We provide for the occasion the keys our daughters must seek to open the door to the next level for a successful marital relationship.

In Plato's ladder of love, the higher the steps, the more intellectual things appear; as Diotima[24] explained, the beauty of the mind is more honorable than the beauty of the outward form. Things get more significant and consequential as individuals climb the steps of our ladder. Two individuals come together through a flirt, expecting to get into the business of love; building a family is always an enterprise. A family is a business folks scoff at, and those who mock often pay the price: they go bankrupt.

Suppose I say to a woman she is beautiful; it does not mean we are lovers. We are not even friends yet; therefore, we cannot jump to bed. A healthy relationship must follow the following steps: Flirting/friends/good friends/lovers/ good lovers/parents/good parents. Our daughters need

---

[24] Socartes addressed his speech on love through Diotima of Mantinea, a priestess he met in his youth. Some scholars believed she was a fictional character, but her words could be read in the Symposium by Plato, under the discourse of Socrates.

to understand the key that unlocks each step. Girls must not force open the door to reach the next level; they must always look for the key. The key guarantees healthy progress and gives peace of mind. There is nothing more tragic for a woman to get pregnant before realizing she is with the wrong guy. These steps will help young girls avoid such tragedies.

We are not saying these steps must necessarily be observed; we live in a modern society, and everyone is free to live as she pleases. Nothing is mandatory; we offer these guardrails to help vulnerable girls from falling into the trap of abusive men. As you know, men often want sex and move on; they are not ready to settle down until their desire for sex, money, and power is satisfied; it's an illusion, though. These men cannot waste the time of any kind of woman because some women have decided to build a family. Thus, these steps are designed for conscientious and industrious girls who want to develop a genuine relationship filled with respect and harmony.

Everything in a relationship starts from a flirt. Flirting is one way a man invites a woman for friendship. In the olden days, only men were required to make the first step. Today, consciousness has grown up, and women can also be the instigators of a marital relationship. From the flirt, the two individuals become friends. As a radio commentator famously put it, a friend is someone who walks in when the rest of the world walks out. Communication is the most fundamental ingredient that characterizes this step. Without communication, the young girl should end the relationship because men often want sex, and once they get it, they will move on.

Friendship is the level where the young girl must open her ears, not her eyes. Today, Hollywood teaches them to open their eyes, and by doing so, many young girls get trapped in the wrong relationship. The tool women use in searching for a suitable partner is not eyes but ears; we use eyes for dating and ears for marriage. Women are so designed; what they hear moves them tremendously more than what they see. By listening, the young girl must search for abusive words on the lips of her potential partner. A man who often makes tawdry comments on women's appearance will later break our daughters' hearts. Remember that women often gain weight when they become pregnant. After the accouchement, postpartum marks will be visible on their bodies. In his essay "On Women," Arthur Schopenhauer said women are like birds that lose their wings after giving birth. A genuine partner must be supportive, and the young girl can detect any fraud in the early stage of the relationship if she opens her ears. A woman who knows how to listen will surely distinguish a good man from a bad partner. A good running mate must often include the young girl in his plans, and how he communicates his programs will determine the kind of leader he is.

Physical beauty never lasts; by the time humans reach thirty, everything starts disintegrating in the body. Being plump is natural; being obese is a mistake, but remaining slim is hard work; it's something the body does not know well to do, and when genetics is involved, it becomes an assault course. The human body is designed to put on fat, and some individuals make more reserves than others. In this modern society, where physical beauty is preferred to the beauty of the inner being, women have a lot to endure. I could understand those who want to preserve their bodies, but girls who wish to have children must choose their life partner carefully. They must listen more and pay attention to the words the suitor utters. As the essentialist feminist Nadine, Baroness de Rothschild nicely put it:

"The great secret of women is to listen to men talk[25]."

Indeed, the power of women resides in their ability to listen. Any woman who knows how to open her ears would be able to separate the wheat from the chaff; this process is critical in the future of the relationship. Once the vital signs are spotted and gathered up, both individuals can upgrade to become good friends. Here, the relationship is more delicate, and signs that qualify this level are honesty, integrity, and loyalty. A good friend will not be afraid to tell you the truth because he cares and wants you to be happy. He will not cover your mistakes but reveal them and help you amend them. According to Plato, love is admiration. From that perspective, our future partner must be a person of admiration. We must truly admire our running mates because we lack something they have, and by teaming up with them, we become like them. A good friend works to make the friendship thrive and blossom. He desires that the relationship continue; therefore, he will put wood in the fire to keep it burning.

This statement by Plato is controversial; it is true we don't get into a relationship to change the other, but we get into a marital relationship to change ourselves. Our

---

[25] Nadine uttered those words when promoting her book "Les Hommes de ma Vie," on the set on the show "On n'est pas couché," on April 2007. https://www.youtube.com/watch?v=nJP-1ToSD-k

daughters must pay attention to the nuance; the partner's desire must not be to change the individual, but her ultimate desire is not to remain the same. An individual who marries and expects to stay the same must not marry at all; life is dynamic, and everything changes continually. If the partner has to force the individual out of her current situation, he is the wrong guy; the individual must desire to move out of her condition because of the suitor. As the famous saying goes: "You are the average of the five people you spend the most time with." Eventually, Plato was not wrong.

The tendency to make the relationship holy is the main characteristic of this level. A holy friendship means unique or distinct. If something is unique, it means it's special hence, always valuable. If both individuals work to set apart their friendship and distinguish it from other relationships, they are qualified to upgrade to become lovers. The two individuals must be working on each other to become a better version of themselves. Our daughters must observe to see if their suitors have a good interest at heart for them to reach their full potential because everyone carries a gift. How loyal is the man? Is he honest? Could he stand apart from the crowd? Does he live by principles? These are the keys to unlocking the next door.

Both individuals have become lovers in this stage, and sexual intimacy starts. The individuals have been honest and opened themselves to each other. Since compatibility is the paramount key in a marital relationship, the young girl must estimate and devise a mechanism to cope with her man. Remember, boys mostly start in class three. They naturally have high entropy, making them have a high libido until they become a father and drop to level two.

On the other hand, girls begin in class one with low entropy; of course, there are exceptions to the rule. Compared to boys, girls' sexual desire increases with age, and they upgrade to class two when they settle into a serious relationship. As you explained it well in chapter 9 of the second volume of the book:

"By contrast, woman reaches her full sexual blossoming at about thirty-five, having finally overcome all her inhibitions: this is when her desires are the most intense and when she wants to satisfy them the most ardently."

Man and woman don't have the same degree of libido; it is a fallacy feminists have been telling the youth. Boys start with full speed and decrease, while girls take off slowly and then go full pedal on gas. And contrary to popular beliefs, women take sexual pleasure more than men because they receive the act. Science said the nerve endings in the tip of the clitoris are twice the number of those in a penis. Thus, when done correctly, women will enjoy sex more than men, but men's desire for sex is continual, while women's desire for intimacy is seasonal, as explained in the previous section.

There is a difference between intimacy and sex. A man can have sex and not be intimate with his partner. Women don't crave sex; they long for intimacy, which usually ends with sexual intercourse. Our daughters need to understand these things to help their husbands and offspring efficiently. Since women are designed to receive the act, they must be able to voice their concerns openly. For that cause, they must increase their knowledge about sexuality; we no longer live in the Dark Ages. A relationship is a fundamental pillar of adulthood, and modern society recommends expanding our understanding of human genitals and reproductive organs to be efficient with it. We have been raised to be ashamed of our genitals. It must not be; there is nothing shameful about these organs. However, there is nothing wrong with sleeping with clothes and the light off. Some people are comfortable with their nakedness, while some are not. As you put it in chapter 3(Sexual Initiation) of the second volume of the book:

"There are men who say they cannot bear to show themselves naked before a woman unless in a state of erection; and indeed, through erection the flesh becomes activity, potency, the sex organ is no longer an inert object, but like the hand or face, the imperious expression of subjectivity."

Religion puts shame on the human body; Greek people did their physical exercise in the gymnasium naked. I grew up in a place where the climate was very clement, and we barely covered ourselves. Here is another way to demonstrate that sexuality is a mental activity. Sex has become problematic in the West and US because of the taboos of religious people. Many indigenous people lived almost naked and had no drama. As the Bible said, sin came because of the laws; where there are no laws, there is no transgression.

When sex has become an object of conquest and domination, it is normal that trouble will arise. The European ideologies around sexuality are the problem that surrounds the act. When people reach adulthood, they find mates and build families. Today, sex is about lust, conquest, and domination; it moves out of its original context. Everything has changed in this modern society; this is a parenthesis.

Our daughters need to know that the frequency of intimacy is the gauge of this level. The solo session is hinged on work in terms of income or money and relationships in terms of affection and sex. Men of class three crave sex and physical contact. If both individuals, husband and wife, are in class one, acts of service and words of appreciation[26] will replace sexual relations as a tool to measure the health of the connection. Thus, when the relationship passes this stage, the couple moves to the next step, and the two partners become good lovers.

In addition to intimacy that promotes them, kindness, empathy, and flexibility are three essential qualities that establish them as good lovers. It is where they tie the knot. Once these three qualities are checked and confirmed, the two individuals are ready to tie the knot to become parents.

Adults marry, not children. Knowing that marriage is two different stories clashing in a tiny portion of land called a house, our daughters must not waste time with boys. The risk is too much for a girl mindful of family life to waste her time with boys. Boys and girls are not on the same clock, and our daughters must never forget that. And when they partake during a frolic, the woman always carries the consequences in her flesh. Life becomes more difficult if a girl gives a child to a man who does not want it. The more our daughters know about reality, the better their existence will become. Here is the sad truth girls must not forget. Pregnancy quickly becomes a curse if the man is not ready

---

[26] The American author Gary Chapman discusses various loves languages in his book listed in the reference. We have done nothing more than distributing his five love languages across the three classes of entropy that exist.

and does not want to hear anything about it. It is a blessing if the man asks for it and is ready to stand by the side of his beloved.

Parenthood is characterized by productivity and time management. In this modern society, three bread is necessary to have a kid; four bread equals two kids, and five bread equals three children. The math here is easy; it's straightforward, and nobody can miss it. If both individuals are not financially and psychologically ready to have a child, they must refrain from doing so. Often, our daughters mess up here. Some get pregnant without the consent of the man. It is absurd to talk about consent because pregnancy is a part of the sexual combo. A boy and a girl who regularly meet must be prepared for a baby because it is the law of sexuality. Sex is designed for pleasure and reproduction. No one must run after the pleasure and forget the reproduction. In the olden day, pregnancy was always welcomed with enthusiasm; it was always a blessing and never a curse because a child is always a synonym for riches. The child would work on the farm if she is a girl or join the king's army if he is a boy.

The situation is different in this modern society. The couple must sit down and plan the event. Both must be ready, and the man must be fully into it. How much trouble could our daughters avoid if they stopped carrying a child for the wrong guy at the wrong moment? Men don't think like women; that's why our daughters must give a kid to a man who desires a child. Pregnancy cannot be free, and things worsen if the man abandons the girl. A man cannot fool a girl who carefully listens; a young girl must use her ears. Here again, Nadine's words resonate:

"If people pay a little bit of attention before getting married, there will not be all the drama we have nowadays."

If a woman is saying it, that means women are missing something. We know men already and how they behave, and we cannot blame them; the game for our daughters is to protect themselves. Everybody will not find a banker to marry, but every woman can spot a man who is not ready for a marital relationship. Boys can play with girls who do not want to build a family or mature ladies who have made their lives already; they must refrain from wasting the time of serious individuals who desire to create a home. If our daughters make the right decision, they will steer in the right direction; the self-awareness operation is crucial for a girl to set herself up properly. Those who scoff at it will navigate in the fog; that's how ships run aground.

Finally, we become good parents when the children grow up to be able bodies in society. Parents fulfill this last stage by giving productive children to the community. Parents lamentably fail in the final step when the children screw up and become monsters, carrying weapons to murder innocent people. Nowadays, too many parents are failing the final exam. The individual fails if her children end up as good-for-nothing kids. Parents are to be blamed if the kid becomes a terrorist or a mass murderer. What is the purpose of making children if we don't have the necessary knowledge and resources to educate them to become able bodies for the community?

Parents must always conceive the kid with a purpose in mind; nothing should be done in this material universe without a purpose because life itself has one. Wealthy people often have children with a goal in mind: someone to bear their name and administer their fortune. Kings have children expecting to give a prince to the kingdom. Only poor people conceive in the fog; most of them are surprised by their pregnancies. A woman cannot be surprised by pregnancy; if we want to change the world, our daughters must grow with a new mindset. Existence is painful because we make it so; God did not break the hearts of parents whose kids and relatives were murdered in Buffalo and Uvalde; confused lads without hope did. If we wake up, things will change. Life is a journey only the well-prepared individuals enjoy.

The entire life exam requires two individuals willing to stay together and get the job done. To their volition, we add understanding; they must comprehend the process of existence in modern society, especially these steps of the solo session. Girls who follow this procedure will not encounter adversity as our sisters have experienced; these guardrails are designed to protect wholehearted ladies from abusive men. Our sisters didn't know these facts early; some reached their fifties before realizing they wanted kids. Many of them got pregnant with the wrong guy and moved through much trouble in their lives; life must not be painful. Our suffering on this planet is unnecessary if we understand the patterns of existence. That's why we toil to open the eyes of the youth because women, very often, gape in awe at their existence as they reach menopause. As you shockingly put it in chapter 9 (From Maturity to Old Age) of the second volume of the book:

"Because as a woman, she endures destiny more or less passively, she feels that her chances were taken from her, that she was duped, that she slid from youth to maturity without being aware of it...... she tries to see the possibilities she has not exhausted. She begins to keep a diary; if she has understanding confidantes, she pours her heart in endless conversations; and she ruminates her regrets, her grievances, all day and all night. Just as the young girl dreams of what her future will be, she recalls what her past could have been; she remembers the missed occasions and constructs beautiful retrospective romances."

I am asking what life could be like if children were well-trained. Instead of regretting, people could have lived indeed if they had known the reality of existence. Don't you think we have an obligation to open our daughters' eyes?

Your compatriot Nadine does not have such regrets. One would say she married a banker; oh well! Oprah Winfrey, Angela Merkel, and many other successful women didn't marry a banker. Moreover, Nadine was a successful actress before meeting a banker, and if she hadn't married a wealthy man, she would have made it brilliantly as a great writer and actress. A man didn't make her; her knowledge and understanding of reality helped her navigate the meanders of life. The youth needs a deep understanding of the reality of life on planet Earth. Things are not working because too many people don't have their feet on the ground, and those who admit that Nature has imposed women unfairly are set up to make it successfully. Women who regret are often those who live in denial, but the imposition of time upon women is real. However, there is good news: life on Earth only lasts 120 years, and sometimes, we come back for another round; we are just unaware of it.

Finding one's partner is truly a challenge in this modern society. Our daughters must be aware that there is no man on the island of Hokkaido in Japan whom God said might be their husband; potential partners exist within a cloud of probability. The closer the individuals get in frequency, the better. There are many ends in the body systems; one end matches a specific individual for a particular purpose. Pierre Curie played one particular role in the life of Marie Sklodowska; another man would have yielded another result. That's why it is so important to know where one is going. It was Michelle that brought Obama to the White House; another combination would have flopped. All couples don't have the same impact and cannot yield the same result; while components of some couples cancel each other, some add their forces and grow in magnitude. The individual must bear in mind the goal she wants to achieve in this life to find the right partner; a wrong combination will never open the coveted door. Those who set themselves correctly will not miss the target. Not everybody wants to achieve something, though; some folks just want to live, move through life, pay bills, and go. These people don't need to break their heads; life is a choice.

Finding an ideal partner did not pose many problems in the olden days because marriage was made through alliances. In erstwhile society, families often arranged marriages, and the phenomenon was more interest-driven than romance because ancient people knew life was exclusively challenging. In the Bible, King Solomon married to avoid war. He frequently married the daughters of his rival kings; hence, he reigned peacefully without fighting bloody battles.

In the European Middle Ages, different kingdoms married princes and princesses to weave strong alliances and avoid war. Today, the scenario is different; the equation does not change, but we shift our mindset. Life remains a challenge, but people live it as if all trouble has vanished. Nobody cares because different governments make empty promises to their population. Our daughters must be aware of the new reality because women carry pregnancies. Existence can get much more complex if they ignore their immanence states.

Nowadays, two fundamental ways exist to bring a man and a woman into a marital relationship. In addition to the traditional arrangement made by parents, we can distinguish a novel method called chemical-based love. The old method was known as will-based love because people often made choices based on their volition; parents made the decision. Nobody cared about people's feelings in the olden days; marriage was a serious business.

Chemical-based love is the preferred way almost all individuals desire to get into a marital relationship in this modern society. As the name shows, everything operates based on the chemical in our body systems. Love falls upon us out of the blue, and we start feeling good. It does really feel good to be in love; everybody wants it. The good news with this method is that nobody works for it; things work independently, and we are happy without knowing the reason. A cocktail of hormones pours into our body and hijacks the individual's thinking ability, hence the expression "love is blind." And we live in a state of euphoria.

The individual seems to be under a spell. They continually long to see each other; they enjoy each other's company, and life appears superb. Almost every human, men and women alike, vividly longs to experiment with this love; everybody wants to fall in love because it feels good. It is comparable to drunkenness or the mind under weeds, giving the impression of living in the "Sans-Souci Palace." The individuals live carefree in the wonderland as if their challenges have vanished. In reality, problems never go away; they have just been swept under the rug. That's why this type of love does not last.

The second method to get into a marital relationship is will-based love, and it is the most recommended way to build a family. Almost all ancient cultures advocated for it; erstwhile society used this method to build a durable family. Here, the rational mind is at play because ancient people believed marriage was a business of love instead of romantic fiction. They kept reality in focus and made choices according to their interest. For instance, in Nepal, where lands were scarce, brothers shared a woman to prevent the land from being divided when their parents passed away. Children belonged to the females instead of the males. In Europe, where patriarchy was still conserved, the aristocracy married by arrangement to preserve the title of their nobility.

However, we must notice that will-based love introduced something bizarre to human society; I don't know if it is evil, but women praise it in Africa. You loathed it in your epoch; it is the dowry system. Why make a human being an object of transaction in the first place? You said the Bronze Age with property acquisition led humans to conquest and domination. I cannot disagree with you, but the system didn't put a price on women only, though; men also received a dowry. In certain places of the globe, the girls' parents pay the groom, or a gift, often in cash, is given to the bride by her family to maintain her lifestyle.

In France, the young girl's parents pay a fee to get a man, but it is the opposite in Togo. Where I came from, the man pays the dowry to marry a woman. In Africa, society perceives women as child-bearers, and since children are sources of wealth in rural areas, people put a price on women. I don't know why women have to pay in France. Perhaps France is a capitalistic society, but the dowry system has existed since the Middle Ages or even earlier; on that, we can rule out capitalism. The arguments you developed about the topic are convincing, but I believe no human being could ever be the subject of any monetary transaction.

Chemical-based and will-based love are the two fundamental ways humans get into a marital relationship. The former is modern and very popular among the youth, but it is the most uncertain due to the trend of our economic system. The latter is disappearing; it is the old way our ancestors used and is still recommended by human tradition and religion today. I prefer it to the other one because it matches our reality. Marriage is not a luxury; it is about responsibility. We marry to take down the challenges of life.

As the old society believed, the husband governs, the wife administers, and the children obey. Today, we can say that the pilot governs, the co-pilot administers, and the children obey. Human society has evolved, and we must adapt. Nowadays, the pilot can be a woman or a man; society is no longer gender-based because some women are more financially stable than men.

The modern family is no longer gender-based but function-based. Since we cannot have two captains in the same boat, one must necessarily be in command; there must be an authority in the house to avoid children stepping into rebellion. The pilot and the co-pilot must work together as a team to govern and administer the house. The co-pilot must back the voice of the pilot all the time. In case of disagreement, they must retire behind closed doors to solve the discrepancies; I advocate for this new model for our youngsters. It allows the best and the most skilled of the two partners to be in control of the house. Men are not always wise, and we need a visionary to maintain a positive balance of the family business every year. Marriage is a business of love, and every company must avoid bankruptcy.

The house's authority should be firm in this model, while the co-pilot is flexible. It does not matter who stands as the authority. By default, the role falls in the hands of the pilot, who used to be men, but nowadays, we have adapted to the change; women can also be pilots. The pilot can delegate the co-pilot if he wants. If the co-pilot takes the position of authority, the pilot must back her. I use the traditional model of a male pilot and a female co-pilot to avoid confusing our daughters. Many women begin to understand that marriage is about responsibility; not every woman wants to get pregnant and continue working eight-hour shifts five days a week. The old feminism puts women in a precarious state. I advocate for a function-based family system instead of a gender-based model. A boat without a pilot cannot reach its destination; one of the parents must be a figure of authority in the house.

Nowadays, families fall apart because both the husband and the wife are flexible in their roles. Nobody is of authority in the house, and the kids think everything is allowed. They fear nobody because they see no sign of governing power in the house. Sometimes, parents have to beg their children to take out the garbage. Kids' role in the house is to obey; they are there to learn and be prepared for the solo session. If the youth understand this new model, they can avoid the trap our parents fell into with rebellious teenagers. It is unacceptable that parents beg their children to get something done in the house; this situation often occurs because nobody has authority in the place. Rebellion occurs during the training session because the environment allows it.

Psychologists often distinguish four parenting styles: authoritarian, permissive, authoritative, and neglectful. The game here is not to be authoritarian because the kid carries his own information. We come to this world loaded; we have talents embedded in our DNA, and one of our jobs is to discover our gifts and serve our communities. If Bill Gates' parents were authoritarian, they would have robbed the world of such achievement; imagine the world without Microsoft products! The story reports his father wanted him to study law, but the young Bill was fascinated by computers, and we know the result today. Parents must be flexible enough to allow the kid to develop his program because every human being is born with one. It might sound absurd, yet it is true. Everyone is gifted; people don't take the time to observe their lives. They are too busy in a bustling world.

Neglectful parents don't understand why they have kids. Those who are permissive don't understand the society humans have built. Authoritative parents are up to the game; they know that the child is in apprenticeship and will fly solo one day. They engage in the training of the kid and monitor her performance.

However, in this schema, our model proposes the supple parent must be closer to the kids, as a friend. A friendship between parents and children normally settles when the kids gain autonomy and move out of the house, but an early relationship can be developed between one parent and the kids to avoid finding confidence outside. In this tumultuous world, continually metamorphosing, one parent must have a strong connection with the kids. Otherwise, they will run outside to seek advice, and we know the outcome. Most children receive sexual education from their friends; thus, we propose that one parent befriend the kids to develop trust and confidence. Children don't open up to their parents because they are not friends. If parents befriend children during the training session, nobody will be of authority in the house, and rebellion could erupt. We advocate using a carrot and stick approach: one parent stands for the carrot while the other represents the stick.

As we have seen, adulthood is exclusively challenging and is hinged on work and relationships. Sex is important in the lives of adult humans; our species practice sex for pleasure. For that cause, sexual education must not be neglected. Today, sex is still taboo; ironically, it is available everywhere. It takes one click on a smartphone to get sex, yet we still treat it as taboo. This hypocrisy is ungraspable.

Sex is medication, and our kids must be aware of it. The youth do not need it because their body systems are still undeveloped. Our children may look like adults, but their minds are still maturing. Early sex is not a good thing, and the statistics show that most girls who start early often regret it. People start sex at fourteen and get done by the time they reach forty-four; it is a misuse of the function of our genitalia. They are not designed that way. One of the roles of sexuality is to lower entropy that keeps building in the body systems throughout the day. It increases as we age, hence sexual love to keep it in control. Notice that we die failure to control our entropy. Whenever degradation outruns synthesis in the body, the system loses balance, and we die. Thus, to avoid premature death, the mind continually manages the chaos in the body.

Children must understand the purpose of their genitalia between their legs, when to use them, and how. That's the job of the parent who takes the flexible role. The co-pilot must be the kids' confidant and friend; the children must not be afraid to discuss with her. They must be able to voice any concern as they would do with their school comrades. If they understand the purpose of sexuality, they will not be in a hurry. The reason why most adolescents want to have sex is that society says it is okay. Hollywood teaches them that they can do it and sex is what youngsters need to calm themselves. And most parents are confused, although they know it is wrong because they have been through it. Some parents had a bad experience and did not want their kids to move through the same issue but lacked the necessary skills to teach them. Thus, some become authoritarian.

Often, parents want their children to succeed. They are ready to sacrifice for their kids, but too many parents don't understand the society we have built. They struggle to grasp the constitution of human beings. Since men are too busy, women can study these things to educate their progeny accordingly; thus, we open to our daughters and elucidate the phenomenon.

In this authoritative model based on Diana Baumrind's work[27], the pilot must stand as the law enforcement officer in the house while the co-pilot is the kids' advocate. Both parents must collaborate unbeknownst to the kids; the one who gains the children's trust must always support the one who stands as the stick and continually praises him. In that game, the co-pilot has an authority that backs her, which she could call at any time to bring order into the house when the kids tend to misbehave. At the same time, the kids have someone to fear and someone to trust. This model only works if the two parents love each other and live harmoniously. It will be a disaster if the parents hate each other. In case of trouble, children will side with the carrot (co-pilot) and perceive the stick (pilot) as a monster.

I advocate for this model because I don't believe in divorce. We don't marry with self-love; love is the primary motive that drives us into a marital relationship. Love gives, forgives, and serves; we can never divorce someone we intend to serve. Separation occurs in an abusive relationship; remember, self-love takes, uses, and forgets. Obviously, two individuals who expect to use each other will end up in divorce because one will be better than the other. The lesser manipulator will seek a way out of the prison they have built for themselves. How can someone whose aspiration is to help and assist quit? If two individuals desire to serve each other, both become fulfilled.

---

[27] Here is an article exposing Baumrind's theory: Estlein, R.(2016) "Parenting Styles," Encyclopedia of Family studies; University of Haifa, Israel

Thus, this model is the epitome of a lovely house and matches the original plan the Creator designed. In the garden of Eden, we learn Adam and Eve were co-rulers: the man pilots the program, and the female assists. Today, we are free to switch; the female can direct, and the man can assist. Either way, parents must be aware that a marital house is a small company handled by a microeconomy. Our daughters must not be concerned with the macroeconomy, which is the business of the government. Congress or the parliament is a suitable place to discuss macroeconomy; thus, anyone who desires to peep into the aggregate economy must head over there. We discuss the macroeconomy in the government.

As we know, the marital house is a small state where the pilot is the president, the co-pilot is the prime minister or the head of the government, and the children are the population. The president's job is to preside over the country's destiny; the pilot has a similar agenda for the house. The co-pilot administers the house and makes sure the population reaches its destiny. And both the pilot and the co-pilot must govern the house through an authoritative style.

The aim of the parents is not to make children rich; becoming wealthy is hard work. In America, the Founding Fathers didn't promise us wealth; they guaranteed us a decent and comfortable life, liberty and human dignity, and the pursuit of happiness for all. This promise is within reach of our youth if they understand the society humans have built and the constitution of man and woman. The Fathers' pledge is not a far-fetched dream; if parents hold their position efficiently, things will work out. Life is a childhood preparation; our children don't mess up, but parents usually fail them.

Our observation finds that children who do chores in the house become responsible adults. Our children live with us to be trained; parents must not forget that. They must make it clear to the household; they must explain the different actors of a house and their roles to the kids. Adult life is a childhood preparation; it is a long process that needs to be explained and outlined to kids. Often, children don't know what is going on in this life; some even secede from the parental house without understanding what they are doing in this life.

When I was young, I witnessed kids who refused to go to school, and their parents had to beg them. Indeed, the child does not understand the purpose of schooling. Parents can manage them and bribe them during the age of assimilation, but as soon as they enter the age of reason, parents need to open up step by step on the reality of existence. The co-pilot needs to bring kids along in her daily chores and explain the reality of modern society. Carrying out routine tasks in the parental house prefigures the role kids must play in their own house during the solo session. Remember that the solo session is hinged on work and relationships.

The school represents the workplace, and the parental house portrays their relationship. If we look closely, the sketch is already there. Adult life arched over a home and a workplace. When we were kids, we went to school to acquire skills to make money and seduce a partner to build a family. Naturally, all children have everything set in place for their success; we fail because we are not aware of this natural disposition. How we behave in the parental house prefigures our behavior in the marital home. How we perform at school prefigures our commitment to making the microeconomy flourish. People who fail in school but succeed brilliantly in life have demonstrated they are more advanced than their classmates.

A girl who does not know how to cook would be unable to feed her children unless she hires a nurse. The natural disposition sets the man to venture out; however, with the progress we have made in our society, the environment is now safe for women to venture out. A boy who chooses to be a co-pilot must also know how to manage a household. His father's house is the training ground to prepare himself for the job. The child learns to administer his future house from his parents, so girls often get pregnant if their moms get caught as teens. Children walk in their parents' footsteps; therefore, we don't tell but show. Parents must demonstrate what they mean to their kids instead of telling them. The world is messed up because many parents tell but cannot demonstrate.

Today, everything is set up for the youth to live a successful life. People fail because they scoff at everything, and many nowadays focus on the macroeconomy to predict their household economy. The government is in debt, but that does not mean your house is in debt. Some say we will be concerned; of course, that's why we have to train our children for Congress. So far, what is happening in the government must not affect the state of our personal affairs. An aggregate economy is different from a microeconomy. The government is in debt, but it has its assets also. If the US government decides to sell its army arsenal, the bridges, the roads, the dams, and all the infrastructure it borrows money to acquire, the sale it makes will match the debt. We must refrain from scaring our daughters for what we don't fully understand. Their concern is the microeconomy; they must focus on maintaining a positive balance in managing the marital home. Why am I bothering you with Americans' reality? American women loved your book, and feminists set it up as their Bible. Of course, you are aware of it, anyway.

Children don't produce anything in the house; they are deadweights and must obey the hands that feed them. They have no authority and cannot participate in decision-making. Some parents want to associate them with the governance of the house, which is good, but they must be aware of their juvenile minds. Parents must not expect great things from their children because they don't know. They are in the house under parental care for training purposes. Parents must be patient with their students and perseverant in their educator tasks. Good parents are those who have hope and can perceive their children becoming. Parents must be convinced of their kids' potential and see them succeeding; that's called faith. If Lady Gaga's mother did it brilliantly, every mother could do it. If Serena Williams' father did it successfully, every father could do it.

I have noticed in modern society that parents often neglect two types of topics in the curriculum: money and sex. Unfortunately, these two subjects occupy more than ninety percent of our adult lives. For individuals who choose to swim in the partnership pool with reproduction as the primary option, money and sex are all that adulthood is about; everything revolves around these topics. Parents neglect these two subjects, and our society is in turmoil. The West and the US are capitalist countries, meaning nothing is free. To get something, one must give away something for it; that's the basic, but we ignore teaching that to our kids. Some people make their life projects upon the empty promises of the government. Officials are ready to sell anything to get elected; they know the government has no money; it always borrows it, yet they promise Heaven and Earth to the citizens.

Happiness is the ultimate goal everyone aims at, although many say the opposite. And no one can be happy in this modern society without money and sex if the individual chooses to be in a partnership. People can be happy in the Amazonian Forest or the Savannah in Africa without money because food is plentiful; notice that things start changing. The arrival of the Europeans brought along private property and hardship; since then, people began to starve, but our ancestors didn't know what starvation was. Nobody has ever died of hunger in the forest. People start starving because someone now owns the forest.

I will even suggest that most parental education turns around money and sex because these are the two things they will look for when they secede from the parental house. Today, our children grow up and cannot differentiate between sex and intimacy. Young girls believe men think like them, and young boys estimate women crave sex the way they do. That's why some of our boys grow up to rape and commit sexual assault against ladies. Nobody teaches them about sexuality. What do parents really teach their kids since they neglect the essential aspect of their education?

The majority of the youth discover sexuality from their friends. A blind man cannot lead a blind man; both will fall into a ditch. The youth need to understand sexuality is for adults, and no one can practice sex under the parental roof. Could young girls grasp this reality and end up getting pregnant at seventeen? How is that possible? Sex and money should be parts of the curriculum and must be apprehended as philosophical discussions in the parental house. A thing that occupies half of the individual's mind cannot be taboo. If we take sleep out of the equation, which occupies one-third of our existence, the remaining time of the adult individual is split between work and relationships. Work is money, and a relationship stands for sex and intimacy; that's the reality.

Parents must wake up to the reality of human existence. Ignorance is playing against us, and the price to pay in this modern society is huge: mass shootings and archaic divorce. Kids must be trained; they are not called to make decisions in the house but must be part of the philosophical debates. Children don't participate in the government of the house; they are the population. Parents don't need their point of view before making a decision because the couple has a life before conceiving kids. Moreover, kids don't understand what is happening in the adult world yet; they are training to become adults, a good reason parents must include them in philosophical discussions and debates to wake up their senses.

An authoritative model with pilot and co-pilot branches must not be an African regime where the father is always right. Children must obey the hands that feed them, but parents have an obligation to understand existence and the society we have built in the first place. The adage says a man who does not read has no advantage over a fellow who cannot read. Children depend on parents to acquire knowledge, but it becomes problematic if parents fail to update themselves. I grew up in a culture where children don't argue because adults are always right. People are not intelligent because they have gray hairs; that's the philosophy of Africa. We often trust gray-headed men, and we are broke. We still offer mud to our kids to drink while freshwater flows underground.

We don't have a philosophy in Africa in the proper sense of the world because we don't hold intellectual debates. We don't question nature, and children are gullible, believing in the elders' tales. Philosophy is the love of wisdom, a perpetual quest for knowledge. The African man has no such thirst for innovation; otherwise, we would have brought rivulets that flow underground to the surface for our children to drink. I know my fellow Africans will be mad at me about this statement, so I urge you not to tell them about this parenthesis[28].

Coming back to our subject, I would like our daughters to know the authoritative model I promote has nothing to do with the African authoritarian parenting style. Children obey but must be part of the philosophical discussion. As they increase in knowledge, from the age of reason to the age of consciousness, they could start taking part in

[28] Readers could check the article where we discuss different schools of philosophy in the world. The paper is available for free download on ssrn.com; Zanou, A. (2022) "What is Philosophy, and is There Something Called African Philosophy?" Social Science Research Network [Elsevier]

decision-making as an internship. They must not forget their status: they are trainees.

Parents seem not to be aware of the reason why they make children. I have noticed how some parents worry about remaking their lives after a divorce. A fifty years old woman would beg her twenty-five years old son before taking a new partner. What is going on? Are we joking, or what? Is it what feminists call men's domination? I see ignorance; a mother does not need permission from her adult son before remarrying. The woman has a life before she conceives and must still have a life after giving birth.

Parents need to understand that all parental bonds are dissolved between parents and children after twenty-one years of age, and subsequently, they must enter into a friendship. A child cannot decide about her parents' relationship after the kid leaves the parental house. Parents must respect them and inform them when they are still in training and living in the house, but not when they secede and gain independence. Parents must be aware that bringing a kid into this world puts some responsibilities upon their shoulders. While the child must obey them, they must also respect the kid. A child has never asked to be born; parents must be ready before conceiving. The constitution of the family must be maintained until the child gains independence, and when parents plan to amend it prior, they must discuss it with their kids. Children have the right to say something about the amendment of the constitution of the house, and that right terminates when they secede and leave the house. A mother who wants to remarry can do so without warning or seeking her kids' approval; it is none of their business. She had a life before conceiving them, and that life will be back when the children grow up and leave the house. Failure to understand some key components of our existence on planet Earth is causing much unrest in our society. If people are not happy, society will not thrive. There is commotion in our gatherings because the individuals are not satisfied.

Today, some parents beg their kids before remarrying. They seek the advice of the kids; why? Parents only inform their kids when they are still in training sessions; the child eventually has the right to oppose his parents' move when he is still in the house. After he grows up and moves out, all parental bonds must be dissolved and metamorphosed into friendship. A friend cannot forbid us to remarry, can they?

Relationships between man and woman must not be an assault course. Things are not working correctly because we often scoff at reality; we don't take the time to understand the phenomenon of life. And our daughters end up paying the high price. Relationships are the most fundamental pillars that bring trouble to women, and our daughters, in their preparation, must invest more into it. A woman must give more energy to her future relationship, while a man must focus more on work. I say it already; we still don't know why things are so designed, but women who often scoff at this recommendation experience a tumultuous life journey. One of the problems awaiting women is marital rape. The phenomenon has taken an unprecedented scale in recent years.

Rape in marital relationships is a topic I want to vivisect; it is a controversial subject, but our daughters need to know. I glanced through it previously; here I come to cut it open alive. Rape, in general, is a matter of ignorance; Outside of the West and US, it is a weapon against women; I refrain from discussing that because the tradition and culture of these countries evade my knowledge. I have never been to India; I do not like speaking about subjects that lie beyond my ken; I am a philosopher and theoretical scientist. Science deals with facts; it focuses on experiments that anyone could repeat as he pleases and get the same result. However, the topic here is philosophy, an attempt to formulate an opinion about a phenomenon.

In the West and the US, rape is more about ignorance than crime, and marital rapes sprout from incomprehension than crudeness. I believe the youth will get over it when they understand the mechanism that leads to sexual assaults in a matrimonial house. I have said it multiple times and will repeat it: class one women and class three men are incompatible. The first step leading to marital rape lies here.

Marriage is a business of love hinged on the practice of love and child-rearing. I want to linger a little bit on lovemaking. Sexual love is crucial in a marital relationship; it determines the health of the marriage. Couples who cannot make love often are more likely to divorce. Sex produces certain chemicals in the body systems that hook and connect the individuals.

Today, society tends to cancel men's personalities, causing their sexual libido to drop. Consequently, some women begin to cheat in response to the dysfunction. A woman who cannot receive genuine attention and affection from her husband will be tempted to cheat if the opportunity shows up. Modern society is full of sexual imageries and contents that arouse the individual continually; for that cause, men must refrain from neglecting their wives. The Bible expressly recommends men love their wives; the recommendation was made for a purpose.

Having a man in his functional personality is better than having a mollusk in bed. A sane woman who is upright in her mind will always appreciate a man performing in his natural role. Women who were traumatized in their lives would complain about their husbands; as you nicely put it, they feel trespassed upon in their flesh once penetrated. Sexuality is weird, and we must not make a drama out of it; that's why people should marry following the scale of compatibility. Two individuals who are not compatible cannot make it.

In the second volume of your masterpiece, you claimed something horrible about women's sexuality. Is female sexuality a humiliation? Isn't this an exaggeration? Let me refresh your memory, dear Madame; you said Adler described female sexuality as follows:

"From childhood on, the notions of superiority and inferiority are among the most important; it is impressive to climb high in trees; heaven is above the earth, hell is below; to fall, to go down is to fail, and to go up is to succeed; in wrestling, to win is to force the opponent's shoulders down to the ground. Now, the woman lies in the posture of defeat; worse, the man rides her as he would an animal subject to bit and reins."

If we don't carefully watch our language, we will trigger a conflict between men and women; the past combat that you pretended happened between men and women was incorrect. Women had never been in battle with men, and you knew it. Today, women capitalize on these kinds of assertions to create unnecessary drama in the matrimonial house. Humans are animals like others, and several of our behaviors are bizarre. Do queens and princesses poo? As surprising as that could sound, people sometimes ask this stupid question. Of course, queens have a shit, and they don't defecate gold. Someone asked on social media do celebrities poop? Their feces are like everybody's; it is nasty and foul-smelling. Every human eats; we all enjoy a good meal, and several hours later, what comes out is no more pleasant; that's the reality of life.

The way Adler describes female sexuality brings horror into the minds of our daughters. If we continue suppressing men's nature, society will collapse later. There is something I want to explain about the constitution of both men and women; it's called personality, and I missed delving into it in the previous section. Today, many people confound personality and character, and some tend to attribute personality to animals. I want to clarify these concepts for our daughters so that they may understand why men behave the way they do; this is not an excuse for men's behavior but an attempt to explain what society does not understand.

There is a person in human beings. When the baby is born, this person does not express himself until the newborn takes his first breath. Something is in the first breath science has not figured out yet; that thing carries the vital energy. As the newborn breathes, the air moves into the lung, and its molecules are loaded upon the blood cells. The blood reaches the heart to synchronize the myocardium and modulate the frequency accordingly; the heart becomes the headquarters of this non-physical entity. We don't know what it is, but the Hebrews called it "Ruah"; the Greeks labeled it "Pneuma."

This immaterial entity is commonly known as the spirit, and because it has set its headquarters in the heart, we call it the human spirit. Every time the heart pumps blood out to the brain and other organs, this non-flesh entity is manifested and projected on the screen of the mind as Will and Representation. In the Will, we have Desire governed by Reason; we have Memory and Perception in the Representation. These are the characteristics of this immaterial entity: Will and Representation. Since animals don't have Reason, they lack volition in the manifestation of their spirits. Therefore, animals have character but not personality.

Humans have both character and personality because their spirits express as a person, a particular state of consciousness characterized by self-awareness, power, volition (Desire and Reason), purpose, judgment, beliefs, and the quest for knowledge. Animals don't have power, although some have self-awareness. Someone could hear this and say, why can animals not have power? Are lions powerless? Let's zoom in on it: In physics, power is the ability to perform work over a period; in this context, power means the ability to do something. For instance, no matter how lions hate hyenas in the jungle, they don't have the power to wipe them out.

Meanwhile, humans can annihilate anything they want on this planet; they have the imagination to conceive a plan to achieve their goals. The only thing that refrains them is their Reason; humans have judgment and live under some moral codes. Animals have no morals, and lions cannot nourish such desire and have no frequency of imagination to perform such acts. Notice that Hitler almost wiped out the Jews; Pizzaro exterminated the Incas. Humans have the power to cleanse an ethnic group they hate.

To sum up, animals have character because when their hearts pump blood out, their spirits display characteristics mainly composed of Representation (Memory and Perception); notice the emphasis. A character is often defined as a mental quality distinctive to an entity; it is a moral quality when referring to humans. In addition to their characters, humans exhibit personality traits. Human personality does not vary much, but their characters are forged over time using Reason. For instance, all men thrive by transcendence; that's how the person we call man is designed, and the person we call woman functions by immanence. The character comes to groove the person. I don't want to let our daughters in the dark, so I provide some examples.

Without judgment and with no Reason applying to the situation, every masculine man would have an erection in front of an attractive woman; that's how the masculine person is designed. Only his Perception and Memory are at play here; it takes a mental image to push him into action. Now, let's inject morals into the equation. By reasoning, a man can decline the offer and say, "No one has intimacy with a woman he cannot envision a future with," or "No one has sex with his cousin." Animals don't have judgment, so they interbreed regardless, but humans have developed a series of sophisticated codes to regulate their societies over time. We can mold our characters based on our volitions (Desire and Reason); animals cannot.

The Austrian neurologist and father of Psychoanalysis, Sigmund Freud, developed a particular insight concerning the human psyche or the soul, which he divided into three parts: the id, the ego, and the superego. Today, the scientific investigation supported by religious books enabled us to clarify these concepts. We know the psyche or the soul is in the activities hovering over the blood; the spirit is the field over the heart. Both electromagnetic fields constitute what scientists call the cardiovascular system. The heart sends the blood to the brain to create the mind, another electromagnetic activity with a different frequency. The spirit is the pilot, the soul is the regulator, and the mind is the operation center. All three fields work harmoniously to generate the inward man or the person.

There is no consensus on defining consciousness, mind, spirit, and soul; scientists and philosophers continue using them interchangeably. For some, the brain creates the mind; for others, the mind exists independently of the brain. Our philosophy uses them interchangeably as well, but in our science, the brain creates the mind because both the mind and the soul collapse at death to become a spirit, a particular frequency of the electromagnetic spectrum. Consciousness, a concatenation of Information and Order, is what is fundamental and could be identified with the spirit. We distinguish pure consciousness from cosmic consciousness, a concatenation of Information, Order, and Disorder. The spirit is a burst in the electromagnetic field with a particular frequency.

Some religious texts identify the person as the pilot governing the heart, while some scientists see it in the individual's mind. Either way, we know scientifically that the activity of the non-flesh entity is divided into two modes: conscious and unconscious. Combined, these two modes manifest in six frequencies measurable in the mind: wakefulness, awareness, alertness, imagination and intuition, and dreaming. The laboratory results match alertness with Gamma brain waves, awareness with Beta, wakefulness- imagination with Alpha, and intuition with Theta waves[29].

The modulation of these frequencies and the individual's interaction with her environment help develop a character that shapes her personality. Masculine personality is governed by transcendence, while feminine traits have an immanent aspect. I define personality as the expression of the non-flesh entity (the immaterial components) displayed through sets of particular behaviors. When the spirit manifests itself, the person is projected on the screen of the mind, and his frequency is expressed in the awareness of the seminal mind.

Men have particular behaviors in front of a woman. You said it already: the soft, smooth, and resilient feminine flesh is what arouses sexual desire. This personality trait is common to almost all men until the individual molds it. There is nothing wrong with a man desiring a woman; our daughters must be concerned if their husbands fall back. A

---

[29] Readers can seek more clarity on this topic with this article: Zanou, A. (2021) "The Mystery of Sleep: The Untold Case of Rest" Social Science Research Network [Elsevier]. The paper is available free for download on ssrn.com

wife must positively affect her husband; if it is not happening, the lady must be worried. Sexual intimacy is what holds a couple together and prevents them from flying apart. That said, I can conclude that marital rape is a triviality.

Rape in marriage is often an act of revenge; the husband coerces his wife as a means of punishment, or the woman traps the man to hand him over to the public. Sexuality has expanded in this modern society and is no longer limited to coition; people flirt, kiss, cuddle, tease, and please each other in various ways. A wife cannot fail to assist her husband in need unless love has died in the house. Remember that love gives, forgives, and serves. When rape occurs, love has metamorphosed into self-love. And we know self-love takes, uses, and forgets.

Domestic abuse does not start overnight; the onset is gradual, and marital rape is one of its denouements. The husband often shows his supremacy and performs the act to demonstrate his power; in this case, the woman is a victim of a series of abuse and humiliation that pan out with sexual assault. But when the woman is manipulative, she will use rape as an escape route. Therefore, she will calculate the situation and determine if she can gain some advantage through the legal system. If so, she will set up a trap to trigger her husband's ego and push this one to commit the act.

Both husbands and wives must understand the biology of man and woman to avoid disagreements, which sometimes occur in the marital house. Humans are sexual beings; it is a reality some people don't want to admit, but the fact is in front of us. Adult life is hinged on work and relationships, which are nothing more than sexuality. Sexless relationships exist, but there are few cases. Humans generally long for intimacy and sex; intimacy is a woman's need, and sex is the need of a man. I am not saying women don't like sex; far from it. I try to emphasize the primary needs of the individuals based on their respective biology. The female craves intimacy while the male longs for sex; we do not know why things are designed in that way, but that's what the observation yields.

There is a huge difference between male and female sexual pleasure; sexologists call this phenomenon an orgasm gap, and it's due to the biology of the two individuals combined with men's ignorance of women's anatomy. The clitoris is the main female organ by which she receives pleasure. Unfortunately, this organ is neglected during lovemaking. I want to shine some light on this phenomenon; the time has come to lift the pall that covers the coffin.

In medieval Europe, the Church controlled sexual activities. The Roman Catholic doctrines penetrated and pervaded the quotidian of the population that the sex life of the society was scrutinized with a fine-tooth comb. The fathers of the Church forbade pleasure, and sexual intercourse was strictly for procreation. They imposed monogamy and banned polygamy, which was part of the culture of many ethnic groups in Europe. This fundamental shift in European culture would become one of the stepping stones in the puzzle that would lead to the development of the feminist movement during the Enlightenment era. Although the clergymen were misogynists, they introduced monogamy into European society, bringing man and woman to stand at the same level because marriage is about consent and can be annulled by women. For the first time, women gained power and had their opinions as valid as men. The religious dignitaries expected to fight the barbarian Germanic tribes' practices by imposing monogamy, but they had sown the seed of women's liberation without knowing it. This situation helped galvanize women to claim their rights later, while their counterparts elsewhere remained in polygamy and never suspected foul play. Even today, in polygamous cultures, women don't complain and see their European sisters as wrong. That's why a woman dressed up in a Hijab in Niamey, for instance, would never understand what you mean by feminism. She never read your books and will never approve of your concerns. She might even see you as a lunatic and a madwoman; it is so because you don't share the same reality. The Roman Catholic Church set European women equal to men; thus, women boldly claim their fair share of sexual pleasure.

Intimacy and sex help determine the health of the couple. The fewer married couples have sexual relations, the higher the risk of divorce unless the two individuals find another anchor to tie the boat of their relationship. This statement applies to the West and the US only because many cultures worldwide still don't have sex for pleasure. It is imperative to clarify the situation to avoid amalgam if someone stumbles upon this conversation, my dear Madame.

Western society has broken free from the dogma of religion, and sexuality is taking its real place in the population's life. The American sexologist Alfred Kinsey's inquiries into human sexual life have revolutionized modern society and liberating women. You knew this man well and could testify how his works had impacted society and gave birth to the hippie movement.

Men's ignorance of women's genitalia and sexuality led many liberated women into homosexuality, although society does not want to admit it. Heterosexual couples don't have the same sexual satisfaction because women are slow to come, while men's orgasm is often embedded in their ejaculation. The study shows the average heterosexual coitus is seven minutes; everything ends when the man ejaculates. The report says average men ejaculate between five and ten minutes. Therefore, the woman often does not climax because she starts warming up when the man discharges and loses his erection.

Based on my investigation, I found the average orgasm gap between a man and a woman is twenty minutes. This gap exists because men don't know much about the clitoris, which is the main organ of women's pleasure. The vagina has fewer nerves because it serves as a birth canal during the accouchement. If the vagina were highly innervated, most women would die during childbirth because the pain would be unbearable. I could guarantee that humans are not the product of an accident as some materialist scientists pretend to be; everything is calculated.

Sex is not working well between men and women because of ignorance. It is the responsibility of our daughters to show their husbands. They have to talk and voice their concerns: what they want and don't want. Sex is no longer limited to procreation; it is also about pleasure, and women must grab their part of the cake. If our daughters do not speak up, the man will not know, but above all, men need to understand that the Bible requests the male to love the females. The scriptures never ask women to give pleasure to their husbands, but the opposite. Women often fail to enjoy sex and reach orgasm because most men come to take pleasure; it must not be that way. Man is designed to give pleasure to woman, and by giving, he receives de facto because sex for men is simple. Men's sexuality is comparable to a modern kitchen with an inductive cooktop. Women are the antique wood-burning cookstoves. It takes men six minutes to prepare lunch. For women to have a meal, they have to gather the wood, set the fire, and heat the pot. The kitchen is set up after twenty minutes. Then they start cooking. With women, the pan of water does not boil. They adjust the wood from time to time to avoid the fire from going off. The sauce always simmers over a gentle heat. Our daughters need to inform and teach their husbands about it. Women are not inductive cooktops; they take time to warm up.

Life is mental and sexuality also. Unlike animals who mate for procreation only, except the bonobos and some few species, humans are into sexuality for pleasure and reproduction. For that cause, they apply imagination to their lovemaking. Sex starts in the mind, and as females, our daughters must be aware of this fact to help increase their chance of reaching an orgasm. Women must start preparing their bodies prior to the coitus if they want to catch up with the man. Men get aroused within seconds; women do not. For a flourishing and satisfying sexual relationship, the man and the woman must be willing to care for and assist each other. Things will truly work out for both if they decide so; hence, some sexual education becomes necessary.

The clitoris is the main organ by which the female individual receives pleasure, and this organ is often more sensitive on one side than the other. It is the responsibility of the woman to know her body, and when she has a good knowledge of her body, she must communicate it to her partner. Men don't read minds, and humans speak with a well-articulated language. The woman must voice her concerns. Sexuality has always focused on men; now that we know the truth, shall we continue neglecting women?

Some sexologists teach women not to aim at orgasm, but they are wrong. They educate women in such a way because female sexuality is complex, and men are often in a hurry. What if we educate men instead? Shall we continue sacrificing women's pleasure for men's sake? I am not a conservative because the manifestation of life is progressive; it is a fact that Darwin called evolution. It is not random, though.

I don't want our daughters to fall into the quagmire that swallows our mothers and sisters and robs them of sexual pleasure. Society has conditioned women to satisfy men, but the Bible teaches the opposite. Life must not be painful, and God never destined women to suffer. Humans, not God, cause tragedy in the world. Our ignorance is the source of our suffering. And we must understand that God designed men to give pleasure to women and not the opposite, and by providing, men are also satisfied because their sexuality is much more straightforward. Life will change for our daughters if they heed our advice and take their fate into their own hands.

In this modern society, people get together for various reasons. In the olden days, marriage was arranged, and things were set up exclusively upon interest. The situation is different nowadays; young people actively seek romance. Most youngsters want to get into a relationship following a spark that flares up in their hearts. However, this way of building a marital relationship often conflicts with our reality; as a result, the couple lacks commitment and divorces within a decade.

Seeking romantic love to build a marital house is usually an illusion because of our economic system. I would advise our daughters to look for love first; if they don't find it, they must focus on work to make money and add a partner. The worst thing to do is to waste time searching for love; staying busy and making money is better. No matter how sweet the romance, the marital house will not hold in this capitalistic society without money. We live in the West and the US, not in the Amazonian Forest, where everything is offered and free. In the jungle, nobody pays bills; trees yield food, and fish swim freely in the river, waiting to be caught.

People who fail to understand the society we have built often pay a high price for their relationships. Most end up divorcing because they ignore the reality and are unprepared. We enjoy marital relationships in modern society through our knowledge of the topic and excellent preparation. Love is a fire, and nowadays, money is the best fuel to keep the fire burning. The youth need to get rid of the old cliché that says money does not buy happiness. Money didn't buy happiness in the past because people trekked to go places. Today, we have planes, buses, and locomotives; companies don't offer tickets for free; one must buy them. Thus, a marital relationship must be displayed differently.

Marriage is a lousy business nowadays; it must not be because half of the individual's life and energy is dedicated to it. Remember that adult life is hinged on work and relationships. Failure to set up these two pillars right is the cause of much trouble and unrest in our communities. Most folks who whine and complain day and night about existence are people who mess up with these two pillars; as a result, their existence staggers, sways, and crumbles.

In the past, couples wedded before having intimacy. Today, the equation is set up differently because pleasure has become an integral part of the individual's life; nobody wants to get stuck with a man who cannot perform in bed. Our daughters must pay attention to this phenomenon because female sexuality is already a conundrum for men, one more good reason that the males of their choice must be potent. Similarly, a virile man does not want to be with a frigid woman as well; high entropy and low libido individuals are incompatible. The good news is that asexual couples exist; that's why we do the self-awareness operation before entering adulthood. Getting to know oneself solves many problems in the future. As you quoted Kinsey's reports in chapter five of the second book, many wives consider their coital frequencies too high and wish their husbands did not desire intercourse so often, whereas some wives wish for more frequent coitus. Alfred Kinsey nailed it: too many women end up with the wrong guy.

It is very important to know oneself before getting married. Too many people are not aware of the scale of compatibility; they marry anyhow and suffer accordingly. As I said in the previous section, class one primarily comprises women who upgrade to class two when they get engaged and start living as a couple. Men are in class three and downgrade to class two when they become a father. This fundamental discrepancy is another additional cause of females' sexual frustration, the primary reason being ignorance. I devise the scale of compatibility to address the issue; it stipulates that same-class individuals are compatible while people of different classes are not. It is well-observed that class one women and class three men are fundamentally incompatible. Lower-class men can cope with higher-class women, but low-entropy women often struggle with high-entropy men. If this one is downgrading, a woman migrating to class two will manage and cope with the man. In case both are stuck in their respective classes, the marriage will be a disaster. Marriage must not be a burden; too many people perceive it as suffering because they fail to grasp the concept behind the institution. Moreover, men and women don't know the constitution of each other, and they end up hurting their significant other.

People often say that you will be a villain in someone's story no matter how good you are, meaning that not everywhere is safe, but the marital house must be the safest place on earth for the adult individual. Our parents' house is the first safe place when we are born. Then, we grow up to build our own nests, where we spend the rest of our existence. Our quotidian will be hectic and sorrowful if our relationship is not cozy. Too many people suffer because their relationships are not well established; this pillar is unstable.

The last thing I want to talk about is sleep. One of the reasons we must get into a marital relationship is sleep. As we grow up, challenges increase significantly, especially in this modern society. The best way to solve this issue is through sexual intimacy. Many people are unaware of it; they move through adulthood, complaining about insomnia day after day. There is no magical fix for sleep other than sexual love. When we reach orgasm, chaos drops in the body, shutting up the source of cortisol in the body systems; as a result, the body drops off.

Insomnia is an epidemic nowadays; some people believe they are cursed for not having a good night's sleep, not knowing that the human body is not designed to sleep alone. Humans are gregarious animals fond of company; they are sociable and prefer to live in groups. The problem is set differently for individuals who decide early to swim in the pool of celibacy. As I have said, these individuals dedicate their lives to God and do not have the same challenges as ordinary fellows. A clergyman has no money worries; a nun does not suspect anyone cheating on her, so she has no anxiety. Their beliefs provide them peace of mind, which is not the case for our brothers and sisters who have chosen to get into a partnership. People who choose to be in a partnership must obey the rules that govern relationships; no one can prime the body and behave as if they have chosen to be single. Existence is not difficult, but we struggle because of ignorance; we scoff at the rules and then blame God for it. No one can marry and behave as a nun; if so, she must live and practice what nuns do: fast and pray. I remember watching a documentary where the woman became an insomniac because she was continually worried that someone would kidnap her baby. The Bible said, cast all your anxiety upon him, for he cares. Our daughters must understand that as long as cortisol flushes the body systems, they will never sleep, no matter how hard they try. It is up to her to find whatever can lower her cortisol level in the body and shut down the adrenal glands. Another easy way to induce sleep is to do some physical exercises, shower, and eat. But we all know what works the best apart from fasting, prayer, and meditation.

When it comes to insomnia, sexual intimacy is what doctors and sleep experts avoid mentioning because our society is still under the claws of taboo. Humans are sexual beings, and no matter how religious authorities held people's lives under lock and key in medieval Europe, the population has managed to liberate themselves. Sex is still taboo, but gradually, humans will reach a conclusion and understand that sexuality is medicine instead of luxury or debauchery. It occupies half of the activities of our lives; we either choose it or not. We choose it when we decide to swim in the pool of partnership. The choice is up to us to make, and we must make it early in life, as early as seventeen or eighteen. Making a good choice will avoid much suffering for our daughters because women suffer too much in this modern society, which is unacceptable.

In conclusion, we must remind our daughters that most people who whine and wail daily in this modern society are usually individuals who are unemployed or have a job they hate; they come back home to bed with a partner they dislike. Adult life is exclusively challenging and is hinged on work and relationships. While women must put 60% of their focus on relationships to get it right, men have to invest 60% of their effort in their jobs; women are most likely to be depressed by the state of their love affairs, while men are troubled by their income and their bank account. Both individuals are so designed because men incarnate transcendence while women reign in the universe of immanence.

Work only guarantees freedom to the individual; whether he is a male or female, work sets us free in this modern society. However, we don't spend our entire existence working; we must enjoy the fruit of our labor. Thus, the individual's existence finds meaning through a marital relationship; humans are sexual beings who crave intimacy and sex. Work frees the individual, but relationships give sense to her life. These two pillars must receive great attention as the individual enters adulthood.

Flirting brings two potential partners together in a friendship; communication lets them know each other and determine if they can build something together. By demonstrating honesty, integrity, and loyalty to each other, the two partners are confirmed as good friends and thus can be intimate. If both are satisfied with their sex life, they upgrade their relationship to the next level and become good lovers. As the two partners are committed, they must check for kindness, empathy, and flexibility; these qualities are necessary to tie the knot. It is at that stage both can envision conceiving a child. Once they become parents, their productivity and time management are key ingredients that allow them to expand the family. Three bread is one kid, four bread is two, and five bread will enable them to have three kids.

Any young girl who understands these lines and toils to remain on these guard rails will surely escape the trap of a narcissistic man. She will set her course up and be ready to enjoy a healthy and flourishing marital relationship. She will not partake in the world's suffering as it used to be for many.

Why Do Women Suffer More Than Men?

A girl cannot be traumatized because a boy has a penis; in the same way, an indigenous from the Amazonian Forest or the savannah in Africa cannot be disturbed because of the features of the European man. The body is not immortal; the person is. The penis is no more valuable than the vagina; they complete and complement each other. Girls cannot envy boys for having a penis; these are social constructs we input into the mind of our children. These scientific aberrations erupted in the nineteenth century with the rise of Eugenics backed by social Darwinism. The Germans are not the apogee of the creation, and the Jews are not lesser than humans. Indigenous people are not at the bottom of the creation.

Dear Simone, I understand your points; you have been caught between the false doctrines of your epoch. These scientific conclusions dominated the past centuries, but today, a Darwinian cannot hold anymore in front of a knowledgeable audience unless he wants to make a fool of himself. While you believe male anatomy constitutes a powerful formation, men, on the other hand, see the female anatomy as seraphic. Both males and females are made to complement and complete each other. After using his physical body to defend the city, the male comes back home to be charmed and rest; how we interpret the world matters. A knife in itself is not a bad thing; one can cook with it or kill someone with it. A baby boy is as innocent as a baby girl;

the problem is how we interpret the world to educate them. Science has done much good work in the past centuries, but there is some damage we must not neglect.

There is functional Information in our DNA, and a conscious being is behind the design of life. Existence unfolds following orderly patterns. There is more order than chaos in the universe, and events follow definite laws; nothing is random, as they said. How do people define randomness? A wise man who finds a hamburger on a plate in the middle of a forest must suppose the presence of someone or at least an intelligent being; animals don't cook. It is time humans wake up from their torpor.

I didn't know what is a black man until I reached Europe. In France, I understood that I was a black man; they convinced me I was black, but I didn't see a black man when I looked in the mirror. Powerful people can make you believe stupid things. The concept of black-and-white has become a prison for us, and since Nature itself is an accomplice, the best way to handle it is to surrender. After all, life on Earth is an ephemeral voyage; it is for a short ride. The main problem with the black-and-white phenomenon is that, only the do-nothing folks from both sides occupy the front scene. You will hear them all the time, talking and quarreling each other based on skin color. They poison the minds of their children.

As you have said, men dominated women, and they made them believe many things to set their hegemony. People avid of power always find their way through, and the manipulation is systematic. It starts early in the education of the kids. Adults' interpretations of natural phenomena stick to kids' minds. Children tend to believe their parents' narrations; it is so because thinking is difficult. It is challenging to think; that's why people don't do it. Today, men make women believe they also can sleep around; meanwhile, women have a different psychology and physiology. I am not against promiscuity, but our daughters must understand the consequences of intercourse: women get pregnant; men don't.

Dear Ma'am, I don't know what you mean by sexual equality, but our daughters must know they are a womb and thrive in immanence. Most feminine women will prefer a romantic relationship to living in debauchery; the opposite is true for men. When offered, most men will prefer to live a life of promiscuity, multiplying experiences instead of settling down in a romantic relationship. The nature of women's eroticism is different from men's. The female receives the male, and people always accept individuals who have gained their trust and confidence in their home. People want to welcome an angel in their house and not a thief. That's why the female is always selective; the male often is not. However, we must admit that men gallivanting around the city does not mean they are happy; it's a pseudo-happiness that does not really appease their hearts. Here is a piece of blatant evidence that humans are creatures of love, and they live to love and be loved; that said, intimacy is fundamental for both individuals, male and female. Men who find love or know how to build it always refrain from a promiscuous life.

I have heard a jaw-dropping story of a feminist who retaliated against her husband's infidelity by cheating on him, except that she came back from her adventure with pregnancy. She called the husband back and wanted to start over. The man eventually returned because they had a kid together. He told her he didn't bring back a kid when he cheated. Women often forget the reality and the restrictions Nature imposes on them. This feminist ended up alone with her two children; only God knows the trauma these poor kids will endure during their childhood. Until parents understand, society will continue spinning on the same spot. Parenthood is everything. Life is not a game; however, if we believe it is one, Florence Scovel Shinn enumerated the game's rules and how to play it.

By introducing dating and the game of seduction in place, men trapped women and enrolled them in sexual promiscuity. As I said earlier, I do not condemn it, but women need to be aware they suffer the most in this game. The statistics show women often mourn over some sexual encounters while men regret the chance they didn't seize. A woman is more likely happier when loved and cherished than the promiscuous one. Women don't crave sex; they long for intimacy. Women need affection and attention. I have noticed in my observations that men multiply sexual partners when they reach success; women do the opposite. They tend to have multiple sexual partners when broke but become wise when financially successful.

Men always have to make women believe in promiscuity to continue the game. We don't have a single father with kids at every corner of the city; we have single mothers. That alone is a red flag and a wake-up call for women. Until our daughters understand the constitution of man, they will continue to suffer and blame men for their misery. We are here to open the eyes of our daughters. They are free to choose because life is a gift, and each individual is a master of their fate. However, we estimate things will be better for our young girls when they comprehend the society men have designed.

Humans are supposed to live on Earth for 120 years, give or take; the majority will not get closer to that figure. And we know twenty-one of those years do not belong to the individual. She lives under the parental roof and must obey the hands that feed her. Notice how some Psychologists have turned the youth against their parents. They teach the youngsters they can also have sex. "If you find a boy you like, bring him to the house," they said. No! It is not true, and it never will be. Sex is for adults, not for the youth. Sexuality has always been with responsibilities; modern society turns it into cookies and candies people can find at every corner. Popularizing sex does not make the consequences disappear, and women bear the outcome in their flesh. If two individuals partake in an act and one must carry the result in her flesh, join me in telling the world that such a phenomenon is not fair. For that cause, our daughters must wake up and take some protective actions. Parents must make it clear to their girls, and the more our daughters know, the better.

However, a young girl who burns too early and wants to get into a marital relationship must build the nest to find a partner. That's what animals do. We are animals equipped with a rational mind. The frequency of personhood separates us from the animal kingdom, but we still share many things in common. We have turned existence into a tragedy because we don't understand life on Earth and how it unfolds. We have erected false doctrines, and now we are choked in them. Our society struggles to distinguish adolescence from adulthood; some call teenage years the messy bit between childhood and adulthood.

Actually, adolescence has never been part of human history. Science and modern society invented it as they do for dating and seduction. According to the Information in our chromosomes, we have two periods of development, which I labeled training sessions and solo sessions. In the olden days, the training session mostly ended with the kid's physical development. Girls transitioned to solo sessions as their first menarche occurred, and parents gave them in marriage for procreation. Boys waited much longer to go through initiation before their parents found them mates. Relationships were about procreation for boys and girls; thus, the earlier people procreate, the better it is for the community. They needed more hands to get the village functioning.

Sex in the erstwhile society was not about pleasure; thus, boys who did not show the desire were not rushed into marriage. Girls had no choice; as soon as a suitor showed up, parents would give them away. In Africa, they used to procreate early, and marriages were arranged. Our ancestors didn't know what adolescence was. I believe people in Asia also did procreate early in the development of the individual. The colossal demography of these areas corroborates my statement. The situation might be slightly different in Europe, but I know that the aristocracy married very young. Catherine the Great and Marie Antoinette were wedded at a very young age, but today, the situation is different globally.

Nowadays, the schema is different because human society has evolved. Modern society and schooling created adolescence. It started in the West and the US and spread around the globe, creating a conundrum for parents. Modern psychology has put gasoline on the fire when psychologists misunderstand human beings. By incorporating the mind into the body, they screwed up society. The mind is not a part of the body; the brain is. This error is the cause of much trouble in our society today; parents don't know where to start. They struggle to grasp the metamorphosis that unfolds before their eyes. Young boys and girls move through emotional crises, and nobody seems to understand anything. They multiply the risks, and those not lucky enough get pregnant, a false step that cannot be corrected. Early pregnancy in this modern society gives the youth an unforgettable experience with a disastrous sequel.

Existence is not arduous; making errors gives it a rugged appearance. A deep understanding and a good education can amend the situation. Our daughters have a lot of chances to turn things in their favor; there is no need to blame men anymore. They can take their fate into their own hands, and we toil for that purpose: shine a light on the problem to illuminate the understanding of the youth.

Today, it is preferable to push the adolescence through and start adult life at 27 years old. The esoteric age for adulthood is 21 years, made up of three times seven years. The self-awareness operation occurs at the age of consciousness that spreads from 14 to 21. Technically, the authority of parents stops at 21, while the kid's responsibility commences whenever she is ready.

University studies are a good reason for the youth to push through and proclaim their independence at 27. With this current economic trend, the best period for women to get pregnant is between 28 and 35 years old. Since the European model is globally in vogue, seven years is enough for the couple to have two kids. Women who want more kids can start earlier, but our daughters must understand that children are an enterprise in modern society. Kids consume money and time; parents need to invest a colossal amount of money into their education and give them more of their time. The world is upside down because we scoff at this reality right now.

The majority of parents are not well prepared, neither financially nor psychologically. Women suffer because they carry the pregnancy, and kids stay with their mothers in case of divorce. Most of the time, the justice system grants women the care of the children because women naturally are better equipped to rear children than men. Here also, physiology and psychology are at stake. A man must provide tons of evidence against the mother to keep the custody of the children. Thus, in most cases, children stay with their mothers. It is not good news because the mother's time is gone. Although she can receive financial support from her spouse, she loses her freedom. That's one of the reasons too many women are so depressed today. We have one life in this physical world that unfolds through one particular frequency; once people realize they have screwed it up, they get depressed quickly.

Statistics show that women experience depression[30] twice as likely as men in this modern society. Life is a tragedy humans have manufactured, but women's physiology predisposes them to depression. The first cause of depression is the environment; the second cause is physiology, and the third is psychology. To begin with, our daughters need to understand how depression occurs in the body.

Everything starts from a stimulus that often comes from the outside. The primary source of our depression emanates from outside of the body. The five senses pick up the signal as a perturbation. The disturbance roils through the vascular system, creating two conditions: vasodilation and vasoconstriction. These two conditions generate two other states in the cardiovascular system, which scientists know as hypotension and hypertension. Finally, these two states lead the brain into poor perfusion, sending the mind into depression. The manifestation of depression in the physical body is known as anxiety. While both depression and anxiety are normal states of the mind and the body, dwelling in these conditions for too long could lead to a severe case known as clinical depression. This condition is no longer a normal state but requires medical attention.

Depression is on the rise because the environment is nasty for women, and their physiology is an accomplice. In this case, women's physiology is related to the narrow domain of their entropy to express. Notice that all human beings have a threshold to manage chaos in their bodies. A

---

[30] This paper give us a glimpse into the prevalence of depression; Albert, P. (2015) "Why is depression more prevalent in women?" Journal of Psychiatry and Neuroscience

threshold is defined as the minimum value or the lowest point at which a stimulus receives a response. Entropy in the body fluctuates between the minimum and maximum values, where the entangled system of synthesis and degradation could maintain its balance. This range of values is narrower in women than in men; it is obvious that men tolerate pain more than women; it is a fact.

The narrow domain of handling chaos in women's body systems[31] explains why they are prone to depression. Science proved they are, and since humans' physiology contributes to their psychology, women's state of mind is also affected by emotion. One aspect of women's psychology depends on their relationships, and women are more likely to be depressed by the state of their love affairs than men. It is so because women are wired for intimacy while men seek sex. While men bring their brains into the relationship, women jump into it with their hearts; that's why they often have broken hearts. Women crave affection and attention; men long for sex. This phenomenon could be explained by the rate of sexual assaults we have in our communities. Men don't complain about it; women do, and they have more trauma related to sexual issues than men.

The environment is women's primary source of depression because of their immanence condition, while men thrive by transcendence. Women interiorize while men

---

[31] Readers who want to know more about the domain of the definition of entropy inside womens' body systems can check out the following paper; it is free for download on ssrn.com; Zanou, A. (2021) "Why Do Women Experience Dissociation When Facing Sexual Aggression and Rape?" Social Science Research Network [Elsevier]

externalize; thus, men find happiness in the environment's challenges. For instance, war is horrible, but men keep doing it; some are even happy to go to war because of looting, raping, and pillaging. Some are satisfied in the combat zone because of the stream of adrenaline that can flush their body systems. Making an expedition to unknown terrain is dangerous, yet men continue to venture out and defy the wilderness. We can say men thrive better amid chaos. As we have said, his Representation is displayed as chaos, while women see beauty and harmony. On balance, the more people understand the constitution of human beings and the society we have built, the quicker we can solve the problems of depression and anxiety.

There is an incredible mental health epidemic going on worldwide. In his book "The Future of the Mind," Professor Michio Kaku reports the thoughts of the neuroscientist Henry Markram, professor at the Ecole Polytechnique de Lausanne in Switzerland, as follows:

"There's not a single neurological disease today in which anybody knows what is malfunctioning in this circuit-which pathway, which synapses, which neuron, which receptor. This is shocking."

It is truly shocking how depression and mental illnesses, in general, eludes scientists. Science has achieved great things; however, there are still many things we don't know yet. The understanding of human beings has slipped through our hands; scientists have made one fundamental error that is blocking us from making a giant leap forward: incorporating the mind into the body. The mind is not a part of the body; the brain is. The brain is our biggest asset, but nothing is more valuable in the body than the functional Information we carry in our DNA. Since then, we have been neglecting this Information, but the time has come to pay close attention to the program that controls our lives. Thus, another particular aspect of depression hides behind the physiology menu I want to uncover for our daughters. This source of depression is the most common and involves our genetic material.

Whenever the functional Information inside our body expresses itself, it builds our bodies that create our lives accordingly. The gene expression encodes for proteins that make body tissues for a purpose. The goal of the individual is to stay in alignment with his Information. Depression is more likely to occur when the individual moves in one direction, whereas his gene expressions push him in the opposite direction. Our desires are not always aligned with the Information we carry in our DNA. For instance, Bill Gates' father wanted his child to be a lawyer, but Bill's dominant Information is computer processing; his brain is wired to understand how computers work. These two career pathways are opposed; Bill might attempt to be an attorney, and he would be the most miserable lawyer in America. Luckily, he was wise to reject his father's injunction to pursue his heart's desire. Many people find themselves in this particular situation where the Information in the DNA does not follow the individual's aspiration.

Michael Jackson thrived in the music industry because he stood on the pathway of his gene expression. When genes are expressed in his body to build proteins, the systems prioritize the organs the individual needs to perform his work. In this case, Michael's vocal cords and some critical body parts received more attention. He danced with his feet, so his limbs were built to have balance and coordination. Bill Gates had his brain wired up a certain way; Usain Bolt gained strength and speed with his feet, and Michael Jordan had vision coordination in synchronicity with his hands to shoot the ball into the basket. The Information inside the body defines the individual if he yields and makes room for it to blossom.

Nowadays, people have difficulty staying in tune with their bodies' functional Information. A greater number of folks are depressed because of this phenomenon, which unfortunately does not concern women alone but men as well. I open this parenthesis to allow our daughters to help their children because parents often steer them away from the right pathway. Their desire must not prevail and stand in the way of life. Nobody knows the Information his kids carry, but we can guess or detect some clues. The story reports that Lady Gaga's mother steered her into the music industry, where she finds fulfillment. Our gifts are made to satisfy us; if we are not happy, we must necessarily go off course. And when we go astray, we will be depressed.

People have various gifts, and we must focus on the one that could bring us happiness and satisfaction. It is difficult for parents to detect signs of talent in their kids, but those who pay close attention will receive some clues because we know how we conceive our kids. Life is not an accident; what we can perceive is less than one percent of the entire electromagnetic spectrum. Many things are happening behind the scenes we have no clue about, and since we cannot prove it scientifically, it is better to avoid speculating about it.

However, we know some skills freely express themselves, while others are hidden, but children exhibit some patterns that could help parents. Gifts always come along with their challenges; we don't know why. For that cause, parents must be protective of their kids; they must be the first line of defense to keep the treasure protected; people like to ruin good things. Folks who fail to lay hands on their talents are often jealous of those enjoying theirs; there is nothing we can do against it. Kings have more challenges than anyone else, and a Goliath always stands in the way to the throne. It has never been easy, but we assert it is doable because we know how it works. Indeed, life becomes easy if parents get involved efficiently; if they stand to prepare their children, the journey becomes an adventure. We believe human suffering on Earth is unnecessary;

Poor people are more concerned by this phenomenon than the rich because wealthy people usually make children for a purpose. They know what they are looking for; therefore, they customize their order. The poor are usually surprised by their pregnancies; it comes out of the blue when the couple is the least prepared. As a result, parents don't know what to do with the baby; the child grows up not knowing why he is born and where he is going. Most parents also fail with the training sessions; only a few know they are training the kids; the majority give it to the government. It is sad but true; the truth always hurts, but it will become a part of us if we dare to accept and digest it.

Dear Madame de Beauvoir, the root cause of women suffering is their immanence condition; you point it out well, and you were not wrong. Men take advantage of this condition because women tend to negate such reality. There is no doubt that anatomy and morphology define males and females, but physiology and psychology differentiate man and woman. Today, we know the mind is not a part of the body; the brain is. The testimony of the neurosurgeon Eben Alexander and the scientific investigations of the psychiatrist Jim Tucker are strong pieces of evidence to support this assertion. There is something alive within a human that moves the body. A man and a male are not the same things, so are a woman and a female. If such distinctions exist, women are killing themselves by neglecting the reality of existence. If humans could be proved not to be solely flesh, then women are laboring in vain.

I do not want to say that men have set a trap, and women keep falling into it, but women definitely are not taking advantage of reality. And We toil to open our daughters' eyes to avoid the trap men set for our mothers and sisters. Life is a journey everyone must enjoy; it is, therefore, unnecessary to have extra luggage. Men make women carry some excess baggage, and radical feminism is why men's trap functions perfectly. Don't you realize it is too much of a burden that a woman is pregnant and still works a job, comes home to cook, and simultaneously cares for the children?

Radical feminism has created a lot of problems for women. The primary motivation of the movement was to solve women suffering, but it ended up adding more, if not unnecessary, trouble to the existing pool of problems. Feminists often ignore we live in capitalistic countries, and they have forgotten that life is currently unfolding in modern society; we don't live in villages anymore. We live in modern cities, and by calling young girls to join the revolt women barely understand, feminists send our communities on an unknown path with dramatic consequences for our children. Unrest and commotion settle in our communities; everybody is confused. And out of this confusion, our daughters are paying the higher price. Women are suffering more than men in this society; it is so because they scoff at the Information they carry in their chromosomes. Our existence unfolds based on a program.; life is not a random phenomenon. Women thrive in a universe of immanence while men operate by transcendence; both entities are incomparable.

A woman gets married to a man; she has a job like her husband, but she is naturally designated to carry the pregnancy. Every night, she comes back home to take care of the house. She carries a baby to term for forty weeks and gives birth in pain; after delivery, she has to nurse that newborn and, at the same time, maintain a job. Is a woman a humanoid robot? What if we start considering domestic labor differently? Could our society make domestic work a paid labor? Why not?

Housework needs to be computed as paid work; modern society requires so. In my pilot/copilot household model, the copilot stays at home to take care of the house. Traditionally, the copilot is the woman, and the pilot is the man, but our model operates as a function-based household, meaning any gender can choose which function to perform. The pilot and the copilot form a team; the pilot fights outside while the copilot operates from home as support. It is time feminists fight the war differently, if war there is. Lawmakers must amend the country's jurisprudence; that's the new ground where the next battle must be fought. If we want to lower women's burden, we must think differently. There is a need to set things equitably in society. Feminists have claimed equality, but they were wrong. Equality is not what is needed, but equity between a man and a woman. Let me differentiate these two words for our daughters. Sometimes, the words we use to communicate are the source of our trouble. Radical feminists expect to help our daughters, but failure to understand their words' true meaning has brought many more problems.

An online dictionary defines equity as fairness and impartiality, while equality is rendered as the state of being equal. Man and woman could never become equal; we have said it already: one thrives by transcendence while the other reigns over a world of immanence. The two entities' anatomy, morphology, physiology, and psychology will never allow equality to settle between them; we need equity instead. The presence of two voluminous breasts on a woman's chest prevents her from crossing the finish line of a sprint race simultaneously with a man if things are set up ceteris paribus.

Equality between man and woman is what society is trying to do, and it is killing women. We have increased their burden because society does not understand the constitution of man and woman. Men and women are not competing; they are designed to operate as a team. There is no antinomy between them but complementarity. By deploying an equity-based program, we will render justice to women and bring harmony to the marital house. Women get pregnant; men don't. This phenomenon alone destroys any program based on equality.

By equality, society expects equal opportunities for men and women, who were not primarily designed to compete.

In contrast, we will destroy barriers that impede both from thriving with an equity-based program. Man and woman are naturally enrolled in an obligatory symbiotic relationship; they are the production unit for life. Man has the seed, and the woman is the soil to incubate; thus, united together, they perpetuate the species. There is no way to compare them, and we cannot put them on the same level as in a competition. Claiming equality and comparing women to men is to match what is unmatchable. Each individual has their ups and downs; man and woman can only be meshed with, combined, and fit together.

Men and women don't need equal opportunity because it will not work; they need obstacles society set up in front of both to be removed. They need an equity-based plan to promote harmony in society. How can we do that? The first step is to remunerate women's pregnancy by considering domestic tasks. Equality-based programs push women to continue working while still pregnant; an equity-based plan will suppress it because being pregnant is a demanding and highly engrossing job in its own right. Pregnancy is a full-time job. How could equal opportunity solve the problem related to women's gestation? Equal opportunity has no meaning for women's pregnancy; it is an empty word. It fails in many situations, yet we continue promoting it. Equality-based programs are doable if only men get pregnant; unfortunately (or luckily, depending on the case), they do not.

I admit and understand when women don't receive equal pay in certain jobs. For instance, men's basketball games generate more revenue than women; it is fair when they are paid accordingly, but national team players deserve equal pay regardless of gender during an Olympic game.

There is no argument that women soccer players on the national team get paid less than men because international competitions have different sets of rules unless I am wrong in my knowledge. At an equal performance, equal pay. The Olympic games, for instance, have a different agenda than a baseball game in Kansas City. The first game represents the country, while the second is making money.

Equality-based programs generate more problems for women because of the immanent aspect of their lives. Sooner or later, a woman will get pregnant; thus, an equity-based plan suggests society consider this situation in advance and arrange for women accordingly. While equality-based plan pays both according to their performance, equity-based programs will adjust and adapt remunerations according to the immanence condition of women. Here is a hard pill to swallow, but if we are willing to build a fair and impartial society, we must understand that equal opportunity between man and woman is an empty word; worst, it lays more burden upon women. And we don't want that for our daughters.

What a life if a woman has to do the hard work in her workplace and come home to continue working without respite? Adult life is shared between the workplace and home; society requires women to perform double tasks with equal opportunity while men are fine with one. A woman performs in her workplace by obligation and operates naturally at home; one mission is too many, and it is the mandatory task that destabilizes the system. And since that was not enough, men have invented independence in marriage; everything is set up to better sink women. I thank God we have a legal system to protect women in case of dissolution and catch up with men. They promote independence in a marital house to satisfy their transcendent aspect. It's sad to see how women agree with them on this issue because they don't grasp their own constitution. Men take advantage of them, and in different places of the globe, some women are sent home empty-handed in case of divorce. Could feminists perceive the tricks in the game of men? Equality is a trap.

Another cause of women's suffering in modern society is divorce. Although both men and women suffer from the dissolution of their marriage, women tend to take the blow harder than men. I will zoom here on the aspect concerning women and provide some clues for our daughters to understand the phenomenon.

The cause of divorce is self-love. Actually, self-love is the bottom cause of all human suffering on Earth; all Christian believers agree with that. Adam and Eve were driven out of the Garden of Eden by scoffing at God's recommendation. If they followed the instructions, they would have demonstrated love back to God. But they chose not to and turned love toward themselves: it is self-love.

Today, some people misinterpret the scriptures, stating Jesus recommended his followers to love themselves, but this is not true. Let's give a good commentary on this verse. The story is reported by Matthew and can be found in chapter 22 from verses 36 to 40, when one of the lawyers of the Jewish elites approached Jesus to tempt him:

"Teacher, which is the greatest commandment in the Law? Jesus replied: 'Love the Lord your God with all your heart and with all your soul and with all your mind.' This is the first and greatest commandment. And the second is like it: 'Love your neighbor as yourself.' All the Law and the Prophets hang on these two commandments."

People often misconstrue the last statement of Jesus, "love your neighbors as yourself," for "love your neighbor and yourself." Jesus never recommended his followers love themselves because humans were doing that already. Every time and everywhere, humans are full of themselves; that's why the world is in trouble. The world will be fine if people love each other because love gives, forgives, and serves.

Humans did not love God in the Garden of Eden; they scoffed at him. They didn't love each other either because Adam accused Eve of deceiving him; meanwhile, he failed to relay God's instruction to his partner. In this verse, Jesus reordered the hierarchy of how love should flow: God first, then the neighbors. Humans put it upside down: they have themselves first, then the neighbors and God last.

Notice at the end, Jesus didn't say, "all the Law and the Prophets hang on these three commandments,' he clearly stated, "all the Law and the Prophets hang on these two commandments." So, which are these two commandments?

"The love of God and the Love of neighbors;" these two recommendations made up the Decalogue. Jesus didn't recommend the love of self because it is nowhere to be found in the Decalogue, and almost all philosophers in human history also agreed with man's stone heart. Human wickedness does not escape ancient thinkers; they talked about it, and none ever required humans to love themselves. They knew humans always love themselves because all human babies are born narcissists. You will never find anywhere on this planet an infant in need telling her mother, "I know you are busy, Mom; do what you are doing and come back to take care of me." The infant cries and gets her needs met right now, on the spot; there can't be a delay. All humans are born self-centered; it is a fact. The self-hate we see in our society is an illusion. Ephesian 5: 29 puts it this way:

"After all, no one ever hated their own body, but they feed and care for their body, just as Christ does the church."

A fat woman does not hate herself until society recalls her as fat and undesirable. It is an illusion to believe transgender people hate themselves; society wants to label them down; people recall that they are less than humans.

Today, we promote self-love while maintaining fake ideologies and doctrines. Self-love has become an epidemic; it is on the lips of everyone: blacks, whites, obese people, LGBTQ individuals, and depressed folks. Actually, these people confound self-love with self-esteem and self-care. The whites need to stop telling lies to their children; the blacks need self-esteem; the rest of the group needs self-care.

If society wants fat women to stop hating themselves, people must stop demoting them. I never knew I was a black man until I went to France. When I look in the mirror, I never see a black person; the Bible does not call me that way. But my French comrades recalled and convinced me that I was one, and I accepted it. I love your people, though; they are funny and make fun of everything. From them, I learned life is about fun, and since then, I used to make fun of everything as well. French people like to tease each other; indeed, life is short, and we must laugh at it often, but America's situation is quite different.

This is just a parenthesis in the stream of my argument to prove the imbroglio around self-love today. Poor people preach it to their children but want to deny it to the rich. Men promote it to be morally free, thereon justifying their promiscuous life. God recommends they love their wives. Self-love is causing more damage than you can imagine. Emmanuel Kant said it could never be a universal law. Kant noticed self-love could not become a universal law when enumerating duties to ourselves and other human beings according to the universal law of nature. The universal imperative of duty said:

"Act as if the maxim of your action were to become by your will a universal law of nature."

So, in enumerating the second duty, Kant related the anecdote of a man who needed to borrow money, knowing he could not pay it back in due time, yet lied to the lender to meet his ends. This man focused only on his own interest without considering the situation of his neighbor; he acted based on self-love and self-interest. Society will malfunction if this man's action is erected as a universal law and gets promulgated. Kant concluded that the principle of self-love or personal advantage is not right and cannot be a universal law[32].

---

[32] Kant discussed this particular topic in section two: Transition from popular moral philosophy to metaphysics of morals, in his book "Groundwork of the Metaphysics of Moral." The version I used is listed in the reference.

Today, society is doing what Kant has discarded; we have almost erected self-love as a universal law. It is preached and promoted everywhere, and people apply it even in the marital house. Couples divorce because they are not practicing love; they are into self-love. The marital house will wobble and collapse whenever personal advantage is promoted within a marriage. Self-care is not a selfish act, but self-love is.

According to Wilkinson and Finkbeiner[33], family law attorneys, for the available data before 2019, the statistics show that the average marriage length in the United States is eight years. The marriage rate is 6.8 per 1000, and the divorce rate is 3.2 per 1000; almost half of the marriage fails. The 2019 census showed a slight decline both in marriage and divorce rates. The marriage rate dropped from 6.8 to 6.1 per 1000, and the divorce rate decreased from 3.2 to 2.7 per 1000. The cause of the decline was attributed to the wisdom youngsters have acquired. The youth has chosen to wait longer to gain some knowledge and get a glimpse of the society humans have built; as a result, they stay longer in their marital relationship.

Understanding the society humans have built is a fundamental step to avoiding divorce. I always remember Nadine when it comes to divorce. I think the youth should listen to that lady often; her words always resonate in my mind: "If people pay a little bit of attention before getting

---

[33] The current statistics come from the website of Wilkinson and Finkbeiner, Family Law Attorneys, https://www.wf-lawyers.com/divorce-statistics-and-facts/

married, there will not be all the drama we have nowadays[34]." The way the youth mate is the problem; youngsters have no cognizance about the scale of compatibility because Hollywood teaches us men are like women. A woman does not go gallivanting around the city; men do that. Women don't rape; they don't break banks; they don't buy a rifle to commit mass murders. Women don't do all these things because they have a beautiful and harmonious Representation of the world. When referring to women, I always focus on the feminine woman, the natural woman without any "artificial intelligence" or man-made hormones messing up her systems.

According to the survey, lack of commitment is the common reason people often provide to explain their breakups. This cause alone accounts for 73%, followed by conflict and argument; infidelity is another big one. These last causes are estimated at 55% each.

The lack of commitment as the primary cause of divorce is one big reason our pilot/copilot model is preferable. No matter how skillful a captain is, he will never reach a destination if he does not know where to go. Every journey must have a roadmap, and the pilot must keep the destination in mind as the helmsman does not take away his eyes from the compass. Therefore, a young lady who stands as a copilot must study the program the suitor proposes before tying the knot. A good husband must know where he is going and be able to communicate his intention. If the admirer is unable

---

[34] Nadine uttered those words on the set of a TV show with Thierry Ardisson; Nadine de Rothschild chez Thierry Ardisson dans "Tout Le Monde En Parle" | INA Arditube. https://www.youtube.com/watch?v=w4yHUPe4KL8

to present a clear roadmap, it simply means he is not ready or does not know where he is going; in this case, if the girl is interested, she can step forward and take things into her own hands. However, if both don't have a plan, they must admit this relationship is exclusively a sexual adventure and could end at any time. Most relationships, nowadays, are predictable.

Marriages collapse because too many people don't know where they are going. The husband has no vision, and most women have difficulty following since he cannot clearly communicate where he is going. In some couples, both husbands and wives govern the ship simultaneously; this method often leads to difficulties, causing the vessel to run aground or capsize. When the husband steers to the left, the wife ordains the rudder to the starboard; as a result, the children are confused, and chaos settles in the house. Marriages lasted in the past because men led the house in an authoritarian way; wives were oppressed but could not voice their concerns. Today, women are liberated and have strong representations in Congress; they have laws that protect them. For that cause, men need to put a bridle on their phallus. They need to control their manhood because a wife will not tolerate her husband mansplaining economics and housekeeping to her.

Marriages are not working because partners are not committed. People are not at fault because psychologists teach them to avoid codependency. Unfortunately, marriage is about interdependency. No matter how they twist the term, the ideology behind marriage is always about mutual dependency. The Bible explicitly said in Genesis 2: 24, I quote:

"Therefore shall a man leave his father and his mother, and shall cleave unto his wife: and they shall be one flesh."

In the marital house, husbands and wives are not two bodies but one flesh. I don't know how people understand that, but to me, there is no ambiguity: people marry to become one flesh. The proof is there because when the man unites with his wife, a child comes out by magic after forty weeks; isn't that impressive?

Some leaders teach couples to be distinct and separate, but the natural law always pushes them together to be one flesh. The survey does not lie; the 73% divorce rate is a considerable figure to make people think twice. Two people who do things together will be committed. If they are independent, they will not be committed. You have promoted independence for women, urging them not to marry. Today, some feminists want to marry yet encourage independence. Isn't that a contradiction? How easily do women fall into the trap of men? Marriage is always about interdependency. If I were a woman, I would not get pregnant with a man for free. Why are radical feminists making it harder for women? What do they understand about life? What is their take on human existence on planet Earth?

Those psychologists who promote such ideology are probably working for men with nefarious intentions. All men desire to be free because they thrive by transcendence. No one is committed and, at the same time, looking elsewhere; the Bible says he that puts his hands to the plow and looks back is not fit for the kingdom of God. A man cannot love his wife and has a mistress outside on her back; love gives, forgives, and serves. The West and the US promote monogamy and stand legally against polygamy. However, a man who wants polygamy is free to live as he pleases because we live in a free country; the Mormons are polygamous communities. Men must refrain from perjury because when one says "I do," he must mean it. Marriage is two individuals intermingling to become one flesh; they are interdependent.

Another source of women's suffering is sexual harassment, and here also, radical feminism gets it wrong. We have devised seven steps our daughters must take to clear the imbroglio related to sexual harassment. The way of a man toward a woman must not be tricky; if it is uncertain, the man is not probably ready. It is normal for man and woman to desire each other, and there is no fantasy or game to make one's intention known to the other.

Sexual harassment often occurs because our society promotes dating and seduction, which are modern inventions. Some psychologists say seduction is part of the animal's game during the mating season, but they forget that humans are more than animals. Humans are persons; they are also animals, but having volition, imagination, and intuition separate them from the animal kingdom. Darwinism puts humans together with animals; thus, whatever belongs to animals is applied to humans de facto; as a result, scientists mess up human life.

If we redefine our society, sexual violence against women will stop. Women need to understand that all sexual harassment follows almost the same pattern and to solve the problem, we must set up a standard procedure and teach our daughters. Everything starts with a flirt that develops over time because the woman allows it. From a legal perspective, sexual harassment occurs based on repetitive actions. For that cause, women must react against the second flirt. We are creatures of habits, and society allows married individuals to wear a ring. At the second flirt, the woman must show off her ring. To the third flirt, she must open up and say "no." To the fourth, "no, I will tell someone," and she eventually tells a co-worker or someone after the fifth action is reproduced.

During the investigation, police officers or the investigator, whoever he may be, must search for these sequences: No- No, I will tell someone- Eventually, tell someone. Without these patterns, the credibility of the woman must be in doubt. We need to pacify our society; men and women are not foes.

Nowadays, many women crave attention because they lack it from their husbands, and many seek what they miss at home in the workplace. People need to understand that sex is crucial in the life of humans, especially those individuals who choose the pool of partnership. For that cause, we are called to marry before entering adulthood. Technically, we are at fault when we stay single in this modern society. Single people must refrain from causing prejudice toward married individuals; we wear a ring for a purpose. A married woman must not be ashamed of her ring; she must display it openly.

Women must understand that men crave sex because of their physiology. For that cause, an adult man who refuses to marry is already at fault in society unless he chooses to swim in the celibacy pool; in that case, he will be a clergyman or a monk, and we know these people are not supposed to get involved in sexuality (a failed man cannot marry though;

at least he can have a mate but must refrain from fathering kids). We don't date, and women must recall that to men. Their responsibility is to prevent sexual harassment from spreading; many of them allow the situation to develop for the simple reason that they crave attention and affection. They lack these things from their spouses and seek them elsewhere.

Harassment persists in our society because of the lies we keep telling each other. Men long for sex, and women thirst for attention and affection; both individuals don't have the same primary aspiration. If they do, there will not be trouble. Relationships between man and woman must be transparent and unfold without codes. I don't want to say people in Saudi Arabia understand the phenomenon better, but the West and the US say they are enlightened, so they must shine the light. In places where women are covered, men are honest and openly proclaim that they cannot resist feminine beauty, so they conceal their ladies. These men admit their sexual rapaciousness and cover women to avoid being tempted. Men in the West and the US say they are strong, but in reality, they are not because our society always has problems. Right now, there is unrest in Western society; it seems like the fool is intelligent while the wise appear like a fool. Women in Saudi Arabia do not complain about sexual harassment. Men and women must wake up in the West to address the issue.

Another lie we tell our kids is that humans are into the game of seduction like animals; we don't do such a thing. If women continue playing the game of men, they must stop complaining. Our ancestors never seduced our mothers because marriage is about responsibility; it is not a game. By accepting being seduced, women open the game for men to play. They need to understand that physiology and psychology play a role in our lives; we cannot ignore these facts. Most feminists tend to ignore these realities. Why do we continue breaking our heads over an issue that is easy to solve? Who takes advantage of the trouble? Someone or some people must be taking advantage of the commotion in our cities; that's why we continue maintaining the chaos.

What is the purpose of wearing a dress with cleavage to a workplace? Women can wear whatever they want at home for their husbands. As you wisely put it, the soft, smooth, and resilient feminine flesh is what arouses sexual desire. Do feminists are aware of that? How many people in our society are aware humans are sexual beings? Do people truly understand what it means?

Life is still a mystery we struggle to decode; until we reach a result, each individual in modern cities must refrain from causing unnecessary trouble. Arab countries have a radical measure to solve the problem: they cover women. I believe society must protect everyone's freedom; hence, covering women violates their rights, but they don't have an issue with sexual harassment. In the West and the US, where we have more freedom, some individuals tend to abuse it; women are stepping out of the limit in their quest for revenge. As invoked in the book, women use their strength to draw males into the solitude of separation and the darkness of immanence. The statement continues as follows in the first chapter of the last part of the first volume:

"She is the mermaid whose songs dashed the sailors against the rocks; she is Circe, who turned her lovers into animals, the water sprite that attracted the fisherman to the depths of the pools. The man captivated by her spell loses his will, his project, his future; he is no longer a citizen but flesh, slave to his desires, he is crossed out of the community, enclosed in the instant, thrown passively from torture to pleasure; the perverse magician pits passion against duty, the present against the unity of time, she keeps the traveler far from home, she spreads forgetfulness."

Do women know the torment they cause men? You have just admitted how a woman can turn the mind of a man upside down. If you know it and agree with it, all feminists are also aware of it. If so, why continue turning men's heads? Why do women not dress up with decency before coming to work? Are workplaces fashion show podiums? Of course, her beauty is her weapon, and she knows yet plays the victim after drawing the man into the mud. Let me recall another passage of your writings:

"The very complexity of woman enchants him: here is a wonderful servant who can excite him at little expense. Is she angel or devil? Uncertainty makes her a sphinx[35]."

---

[35] I used three versions of "The Second Sex" (French and English) to write this book. I often refrain to give the page of the citation because it will confuse someone who has the paper format or another translation. I prefer to give the chapter and the volume whence the quote was drawn. The translations and editions I used are listed in the reference. A good tip to check quotation today is the web: one can get the ebook and type some phrases in the search motor to have the passage. Today, technology has made the job easier for critics.

Women need to be aware of their status and nature. Who made things so? We don't know. Why must she have such an influence on man and turn his head upside down? As if that is not enough, some women threaten to go outside topless. There is nothing wrong with it, but they must not complain that men stare at them. Nature didn't ask women before equipping them with a womb; it didn't ask men before pushing them into transcendence. It seems like both men and women are victims of something they don't understand, and the best way to cope with the situation is to respect one another.

Feminists toil day and night to prove there is no difference between man and woman, and modern society has started teaching our children that women can have a one-night stand, wake up, and go as if nothing happened. That's one of the ways feminists try to justify the new ideology; thus, men adjust and move accordingly as women exhibit the new lifestyle. It is a trap set up by men; it is a lie, and we know it because men don't complain; women do. Sexuality with no strings attached is men's invention, not women's. A feminine woman does not function that way because she normally craves attention, not sex. There is a huge difference between intimacy and sex; men need to engrave this fact in their minds, and women as well. Our society is in shambles because we create the mess out of ignorance.

If we say physiology is not playing any role in men and women, we are lying to ourselves because sexual intercourse is only possible if the penis is erected. The rotor must be rotating for an electric central to produce electricity, and sexual intercourse between a man and woman requires a penis and a vagina. These two organs are not similar and do not function in the same way; they are designed to complete and complement each other.

The urge for an equality-based program is not serving women well because men and women are not designed to compete with each other. Radical feminists, through their claims, put women in competition with men, and men love it because they know there is no match. It is a trap feminists still don't understand. Men convince women to do as they do and push women into promiscuity. If the woman is of high entropy, there is nothing wrong with it, but most women naturally long for intimacy, and many find themselves destabilized by this lifestyle. I have nothing against women's desire to be like men, but our daughters need to understand men don't complain; women do.

We cannot judge a fish by its ability to climb a tree, said a famous scientist; there is no fair selection to test a dog and monkey climbing a tree. Even in the same species, lions and lionesses don't have the same function in the group. Equity-based programs will amend human society and serve the interests of women better. As you put it:

"Man exalts the phallus in that he grasps it as transcendence and activity."

Women don't function by transcendence, and nature puts them at the passive end as receivers; they are the ground that receives the seed. For that cause, she cannot thrive in promiscuity. I heard the story of a woman who lived in promiscuity; she woke up in her fifties to notice she had no child. She regretted how time had passed so fast as she desired to have kids but never planned it thoughtfully. We are not discouraging women from enjoying existence as they please; we are here to open our daughters' eyes based on the functional Information embedded in their chromosomes. Mental illnesses are on the rise, and nobody knows anything about what is happening. No one goes against the dominant program in his DNA and is fulfilled in life. In my investigations that span over twenty years, I have always discovered that happy individuals on Earth are those who live in agreement with their dominant programs.

It is an error to train girls to behave as men do; a decent society always condemns men's behavior. Men often assault women, but today, with feminist propaganda, some group of women has decided to fight back. They prey on young schoolboys; the phenomenon is so common in the United States nowadays that lawmakers have amended our jurisprudence. This behavior is not natural to women, but humans are species that adapt to change, I admit it. As society's rhetoric starts changing, women's behavior has metamorphosed accordingly. However, I was baffled and speechless when you said women of some primitive people had brutally raped a stranger that dared to come to their village during the days of weeding. Could a woman rape a man? How do we define rape?

Today, the amalgam has grown big in this modern society, and people often confound sexual assault with rape. By definition, rape is a sexual assault that ends up with penetration. On the other hand, a sexual assault is an unsolicited sexual act. Rape must necessarily involve the violation of the victim's intimacy; the victim's private parts must be forced and entered. Without penetration of any kind, we must rule out rape in favor of sexual aggression.

A sexual penetration into the victim's body without the individual's consent is the ultimate proof of rape. That said, how can a woman rape a man?

Our communities have unrest because we use words interchangeably, leading everybody into befuddlement. A woman cannot rape a man unless she ties him down; perhaps women in that village empowered the man and subdued him. All things considered, a man raped by a woman would not be traumatized as if the situation is reversed because women live by immanence. They receive the seed into their flesh while men project it. The only moment women deeply enjoy and accept a man's seed is when they are in love, engaging in mutual and consenting frolics. By their biology, women organize the feast; they choose and welcome the man. Often, he leaves inside her flesh a souvenir that a woman can loath the rest of her life if she does not nourish any sentiment toward the man. There is always a risk of pregnancy when a man sets his course inside a woman; our daughters must not be ignorant about this fact.

Pregnancy is the last topic in women suffering that I do not want to sidle past; there is a lot to say here. First, our daughters must know that pregnancy is the highest entropy state in the human body. Although men are notoriously known as individuals of high entropy, women register the highest possible entropy; the second is menstruation. Entropy is chaos in the body; living organisms die when entropy cannot be contained. The Japanese biologist Yoshinori Ohsumi notices that life is maintained by a tightly controlled balance between degradation and synthesis; he means that life will cease in the body whenever the balance is ruptured. From this perspective, we can understand that pregnancy is the most dangerous state of life. In medieval Europe, one out of every twenty women died during childbirth. Today, in this modern society, maternal mortality is in decline. UNICEF[36] website shows a drop of 38% between 2000 and 2017, with an estimated 211 deaths per 100,000 live births. On balance, pregnancy remains a dangerous condition for women. Nature spares men, and they don't have to go through such a trial; they are really lucky!

Pregnancy starts when the man releases his sperm inside the woman during coitus; as the sperm encounters the ovum, often found in one of the fallopian tubes, it empties its content inside the egg. The sperm brings to the egg half of the Information needed to build a new human; the woman provides for the rest, which is not an easy task. To gather all the ingredients necessary to fabricate a baby, the mother must endure a difficult period of forty weeks. This phenomenon predisposes women to be fat. Unfortunately, men don't understand it, and some of them have to drive their wives through emotional abuse. Let me open a parenthesis on this particular aspect of women's lives that also causes much suffering, especially emotional pain.

Fat-shaming is a modern way of humiliating women because they are overweight or fat. The phenomenon has taken an unprecedented proportion due to Hollywood celebrity news, where actresses are depicted as the standard beauty model. Anyway, as the French saying goes, the wine is drawn, it must be drunk; that's why I am here to help our daughters navigate the meanders of this modern society.

---

[36] https://data.unicef.org/topic/maternal-health/maternal-mortality/

Hollywood sets up the pace, and everybody must fall in line. Society shames women for being fat and praises men for going to war. If both men and women have a natural propensity for something we judge vile, why abash one and compliment the other? One needs to be a philosopher to see through the veil of stupidity, and society hates this one when he finally can see through it. You were one of these philosophers who pierced through human stupidity and aberration, and I heed how society treated you. You were not alone; before you, Mary Wollstonecraft paid the price of human double-mindedness. Olympe de Gouges didn't keep her head on her shoulders; she lost it. The French Revolution was a big comedy and blatant injustice against women in human history. I forgive them, and you must also because humans are flawed creatures. I am a man, but I lost my respect for human society when I noticed that our rulers lead by force instead of reason. In the olden days, we respected leaders because they were brave and full of wisdom; today's society is full of men who barely grasp existence. They stand by dogmas and doctrines they cannot defend in any intellectual debate before a knowledgeable audience. What can we say to these men who see less than one percent of the room yet believe that's all that exists? They build weapons to destroy human life and are not embarrassed but disgusted because a woman becomes plump. Saint Paul said their glory is in their shame. Some of them are lucky to be born with a silver spoon in their mouth; if they had to go through adversity as their ancestors did, I do not think many would survive. To these men, Jesus said in Matthew 23:24-27, I quote:

"Blind guides, who strain out a gnat and swallow a camel! "Woe to you, scribes and Pharisees, hypocrites! For you cleanse the outside of the cup and dish, but inside they are full of extortion and self-indulgence. Blind Pharisees, first cleanse the inside of the cup and dish, that the outside of them may be clean also. "Woe to you, scribes and Pharisees, hypocrites! For you are like whitewashed tombs which indeed appear beautiful outwardly, but inside are full of dead men's bones and all uncleanness. Even so you also outwardly appear righteous to men, but inside you are full of hypocrisy and lawlessness."

Women are naturally designed to become fat because of pregnancy. Weight gain is something our daughters need to understand. Doctors and dieticians are beating the bush and struggling to understand the phenomenon, or perhaps they know it but are still making money. One of their doctors said modern medicine profits from sickness instead of health. We live in a capitalistic society and cannot blame them, but I doubt their science. I investigate weight gain personally, and the problem cannot be a conundrum. It is still a problem because the constitution of humans slips through our hands.

In his epoch, the Austrian Nobel laureate Erwin Schrodinger carried out some works on the phenomenon of life; he concluded that life is a struggle against entropy[37]. Therefore, living organisms need metabolism to compensate for chaos inside the body to stay alive. By metabolism, he meant eating, drinking, and breathing.

---

[37] Erwin Schrodinger discusses entropy in chapter 6 of his book "What is Life?" The book and the paper of the Japanese Noble laureate Yoshinori Ohsumi could be found in the reference. The scientific investigations of these two scientists combined will elucidate major problems in biology today.

As the word comes out, metabolism is what our daughters need to understand; each one of us has a different metabolism. Academics often define metabolism as the chemical processes occurring inside living organisms' bodies to keep them alive. In other words, metabolism is how the body turns what we eat, drink, and breathe into energy to keep the body going. That said, our daughters must comprehend how their body processes their intakes of fuel. It is usual for the body to gain weight because it is designed that way for a purpose. Science also shows that women gain weight faster than men, which is comprehensible because women fabricate babies. Notice that women make their babies from scratch. Actually, the man provides nothing more than Information; he contributes poorly to the baby-making process; the woman has to build the baby out of her resources alone. Thus, the female body was programmed to store energy more than men, and it does it with incredible skills.

The physical body of humans often assumes tomorrow is uncertain and that food could be rare; for that cause, whenever possible, the body makes some reserves. Today, people living in modern cities loathe what the body knows better to do; women hate it the most because society puts pressure on them. What we hate today was a survival mechanism that enabled our ancestors to get to where we are right now. Stockpiling fat was not bad because the food was not always readily available in those days; there was no fridge, and humans had not invented pasteurization yet.

The first step our daughters need to take in this fight to manage their body weight is to know themselves; we have never stopped emphasizing this point: know thyself. Two options are available for the individual: she has either a slow or fast metabolism. These two groups of people behave differently in managing their food supplies. People with fast metabolisms quickly turn their food intake into energy; this means the body is lazy putting some aside. This system is a great spender; it blows whatever it gets very quickly, and that was not a good quality in the olden days because the individual would die first in case of famine.

The second group comprises people with a slow metabolism. These people burn their food supplies slowly and tend to make more reserves. In practical life, these people are called stingy individuals; their bodies manage the resources with parsimony; we also call them the miser. However, this quality was the best for a survival trait. I can say the female body is a miser compared to the male's body. The female body is far-sighted because she doesn't know when a pregnancy could occur, so it continually stocks reserves if something happens.

Once our daughters understand the phenomenon, they can act to mitigate the problem. In modern cities, we have a lot of food, and we become fat, so cutting down on food is the first step to take. To be honest and not offend anyone, people nowadays overeat. They do so because many are looking for pleasure in food. Actually, we enjoy eating food; the satisfaction we seek pushes us to binge. And for some, sexual excitement is equal to the pleasure they get when eating; there is a lot of pleasure in eating; that's why we keep eating. We eat not only to satisfy our appetite but also to have our dose of pleasure.

To close this parenthesis, our daughters must understand that pregnancy is one of the causes of the body stockpiling fat. During the gestation period, not only does the woman feed herself, but she also feeds the baby. Science says the blood volume of pregnant women doubles as the baby starts building its own blood supply systems. The mother's immune system sees the baby as a foreign object as his blood system is separated from the mother by the placenta. The infant continually pumps nutrients from the mother, increasing chaos inside the mother's system. Appetite tends to augment to satisfy the demand for calories of the ever-growing infant. As the baby grows, so does the uterus, and all the abdominal muscles stretch to accommodate the change. All internal organs are squeezed, making it harder for the woman to breathe; she has to work hard to pump the high volume of blood circulating through the entire body, increasing her heart rate and blood pressure. All these new conditions make her uncomfortable. That's why a pregnant woman must be treated like a queen; she deserves double attention. Unfortunately, most men don't understand it, and some even mock it. If human men had understood pregnancy, society should have already put a price on it.

The biology behind pregnancy is still a work in progress, and because of the paucity of my present knowledge on the subject, I will limit myself to this brief description. I am not a woman and cannot continue prating on women's conditions. However, I am pro-life, but my hands are not over women's uterus. Everybody knows how awful it is to binge on food and go and vomit it.; some women are doing exactly that. Abortion is still a huge debate in America, but we must not forget the struggle of conscientious women going through serious pregnancy issues. I saw a meme on social media that was attributed to a famous actress; I do not know if she eventually did say that, but the quote goes this way:

"If men could get pregnant, abortions would be available at Jiffy Lube."

It is hilarious and sad to notice how men use double standards in this life; they put women in that condition and play Pontius Pilate. As you nicely put it in chapter 6 of the second volume, "men who most respect embryonic life are the same ones who do not hesitate to send adults to death in war."

Indeed, one must be a philosopher to perceive men's stratagem; sometimes, it is better to be dumb than smart. The situation is ludicrous in America; the more I read and watch different political parties fighting over abortion, the more I am bewildered. I sometimes laugh at the contradiction that often emerges. People who fight against abortion are the same people who stand against universal health care. Those who promote abortion hate guns because they ironically care for human life. The one who fights for the unborn baby promotes guns and cares less for the individual's life on death row; they are so swamped protecting the fetus that they forget to keep little children safe in elementary schools. The pro-life is a believer who worships God he cannot see and is more concerned about the unseen fetus. Indeed, he cares more for the invisible than the visible. If the lives of unseen infants are more important than the living ones, bear with me that they are not pro-life but pro-birth. The pro-choice does not believe in God because he cannot see him; as a result, he cares less for the unseen fetus and sheds warm tears when little children are brutally murdered. I finally adore the way you sum it up: society develops uncompromising love for humans in the fetal condition but denies leniency to the adult individuals. You say it all, dear ma'am.

Women go through a great deal of pain than men; their suffering is imposed on them by Nature, while men create their own suffering. Why should society have to care if someone, on a sunny afternoon, decides to jump from his balcony with a skateboard? Men do all kinds of stupid things, and we know the worst of all is war. Women, on the other hand, never seek their misfortune. Without their consent, someone or something imposes on them. A woman is coerced into doing something she has never chosen, and I sympathize with her pain thereon. That's why I cannot put my hand over her uterus.

Often, people control women in the name of God they have never seen or heard of. If God did speak to them, what did he say? Did God tell them to punish women for what men caused? Frankly speaking, pregnancy is man's fault. Luckily, we have devised a good plan for our daughters to navigate the maze today. Things will be amended once they understand the constitution of their body and how man also functions.

The problem around abortion exists because our daughters are broke and ignorant. In her epoch, Wollstonecraft believed women were ignorant because men took their rights to education; thus, society would be better off if women had access to education. In this modern society, the individual lacks sexual education, both men and women, because sex is still considered taboo. Meanwhile, sex is a medicine; love-making eventually has two purposes:

pleasure first and reproduction later. This statement could irk some religious dignitaries, but let's get a closer look at it.

If a man and woman meet in frolicking, they have pleasure on the spot, and the baby comes after forty weeks of gestation. The two individuals don't wait forty weeks to feel the joy of the act; they have the reward right away on the spot, and only the woman carries the burden of pregnancy. In the light of this statement, it neatly appears that pleasure comes first and reproduction second.

As I have already said, the clitoris is the main organ of pleasure for women, not the vagina; women are not on fire, and men cannot play the firefighters. However, if men believe to be firemen, the couple must keep a strict calendar on the bedroom wall. The stronger the desire in women, the closer they are to the ovulation date. Women must understand their bodies and keep track of their menstrual cycles; it is not difficult.

Pleasure focuses on the clitoris, and reproduction passes through the vagina. If husbands and wives put into it some effort, this problem of abortion will subside. Love-making is an art; it must be. Our ancestors in the Garden of Eden chose the path of knowledge, and we must be good at it. The scriptures said my people are destroyed for lack of knowledge. If science hadn't spent most of its time chasing animals, we would have known human beings better. We are not solely flesh, and the world needs to understand how the non-flesh entity interacts with the mind to create our realities.

Women are designed for childbearing; it is a fact our daughters must not ignore; however, they can be in control of their existence if they understand the constitution of both man and woman. The lies we tell our children are the problem; a woman is a womb. For that cause, she must decide early which pool to swim. Partnership and procreation mean you cannot waste time with boys and broke men. A young girl who acquires good sex education and a deep understanding of the female body will keep herself safe from unwanted pregnancy. Teen pregnancy is off-topic because sexuality belongs to adults; however, a teenager who finds herself burning with desire must proclaim her independence to secede from the parental house. She must carry the self-awareness operation to get to know herself and the society humans have built; from there, she can find a partner to meet her needs.

If I were a teenage girl who seceded too early from the parental house, I would never team up with boys because females are naturally designated to carry the burden of pregnancy. Pleasure is what could push a teenage girl to separate early from her parents; if so, why seek it from a boy? Sex is mental, and no one ever enjoys it when being in doubt and frigid; one must be in total relaxation to have fun, and only a mature man capable of taking care of the outcome could offer that peace of mind. I would urge our daughters to extend their training sessions, but when the individual is burning madly, she can find a partner but must first understand human society. A boy can never be a good partner in her situation because adult life is hinged on work and relationships. A lad with a good plan and a dream is not a boy but a man. If our daughters know where they are going, they can identify a partner working the same pathway. A good captain is the one that knows where he is going. After all, why allow someone to be a captain if one can be one?

The young girl can be a captain if she discovers her gift and works it to fruition. If she struggles to find her talents, she can extend her studies or get trained to get a career. These are the genuine ways to be in control of one's life in this modern society. Human society has evolved, and women can be anything they want; there is no need to wait for a man. A girl who does not want to wait for a man must extend her stay in the parental house to increase her competitivity in the market. The ball is in her court; she must make a good choice. Girls fumble with their lives because many make bad choices, and most mistakes occur during the age of consciousness, between fourteen and twenty-one. Thus, we devise this step-by-step guide we label essentialist feminism to help them navigate the meanders of life on this planet.

Should We All Be Feminists?

The Nigerian writer Chimamanda Adichie believed we should all be feminists. You don't know her; she is one of your followers. You have been a charismatic leader who left many waves in your wake, but the young generation is not as staunch as you were. The tree you planted has borne fruit; the society has changed. Indeed, things are changing but not so fast; however, we can admit that significant obstacles have been cleared up for women. Rihanna, Lady Gaga, Beyoncé, Taylor Swift, Serena Williams, and Adele are good examples of how our daughters can start from scratch and rise to prominence.

One of my purposes here is to explain why essentialist feminism is preferred to existentialist feminism, a school of thought you belong to. I believe essence precedes existence in several cases of our lives and that man and woman have some assigned functions in society. No matter how hard he tries, a man will never get pregnant, meaning the human species forms a function-based community. Feminists' claims sometimes left me flummoxed; they seem not to consider reality. Women are the guardians of life. Although life is still a mystery, we toil to elucidate existence, which, on the other hand, follows well-definite patterns. We must not let radical feminism close our eyes to reality. After all, it is a human-made doctrine like others, and it has its flaws.

Should a feminist accept a wedding ring from a man? This is a conundrum I am still puzzling about until now. You refused to marry because you believe a feminist cannot follow the tradition of men. A wedding ring is a stone a businessman collects from the river, polishes it, and sells it to people at a high price. Can you imagine one of these rings can cost up to eight million dollars? Should we be feminists yet accept these rings from a suitor? What's the purpose of wearing an expensive ring with a stone a businessman collected from a river?

Let's put aside the ring to delve into the concerns of feminists in this modern society. I have to believe feminism is a time-related phenomenon because most of your problems have become obsolete today. Like you, Adichie also has concerns. She does not understand why society accepts men's anger but disagrees when women display the same emotion. Society teaches girls not to be angry, aggressive, and brutal while tolerating or even praising the same behavior in boys. These are the words in her book. She narrated her experience as a woman in Nigerian society, and I think her concerns need to be addressed. As an African man and a Frenchman at heart, I can say I understand both of you.

I am not trying to justify our society, but I am here to explain why things are so designed. The Nigerian feminist must understand that men and women are designed to stay together; for that, we are on the same page. She is in agreement with my philosophy, and I believe humans should marry. The production unit is a family made of man and woman, together in a tiny portion of land called a house. Today, the definition of family is modern, and society tends not to see the division of roles anymore. Moreover, our society has evolved tremendously (I want to believe it), and Vikings no longer exist to storm our cities, rape women, and kill people (It's still happening, though, even in Europe).

First, let's explain the biology behind men's anger. Frankly, women are not designed to get angry; they are naturally flushed with oxytocin hormone, which promotes harmony and stability for their body systems. This statement does not concern American women because the United States is different. If you are a woman living in the United States, your anger is justified, don't get me wrong.

I have in mind a society in a relative equilibrium like Switzerland or the Scandinavian countries; I mainly target places where men don't have an extra Y chromosome and are effective with their rational faculties. I am dealing with countries where people possess guns but are aware they cannot kill human beings in the street like animals. I refer in my analysis to countries where parents are open-minded to connect the dots and separate reality from fiction.

So, I said women have oxytocin while men are primarily flushed with testosterone, a hormone that gives them enough courage to pick up the sword and fight the aggressors who invade the city to kill and enslave. I don't know how a wife would call her partner if an intruder entered their house and her husband hid under the bed. Women always desire to marry strong men. In the olden days, men who were physically fit to cultivate the land, take the sword, and go to battles were qualified as the active force of the city. Those unfit were made eunuchs and stayed in the palace to serve the queen and the king's concubines. Eunuchs did not have the right to marry, and no woman wanted them anyway because they could not perform in bed.

Men are naturally designed to be angry because anger empowers their body systems in the fight-or-flight response.

Warriors don't wield swords with a smile; they must be angry enough to deal with the enemy. Since women do not participate in the battle, there is no need to get angry. Nature designs them according to the role they are called to perform in the community.

One thing is to get angry, and another is to know how to control one's anger; notice that women are naturally designed to help men manage their anger. In the same way, we come home to plug our cellphones into the electric socket to recharge them; men retrieve stability when united with their women. The analogy is gross but very helpful if we look at it closely. When we were kids, we found refuge in our mothers' arms. They gave us their breast to suck when we were crying. The same behavior is still valid once grown up. The arms of a woman are the best place for a man to find refuge. Today, we have created bars and opium lounges, but nothing is more soothing than the caress of a lovely woman. I recall your words again: the soft, smooth, and resilient feminine flesh is what arouses sexual desire. You are not wrong; it does, and men and women know it.

Our society has unrest because we no longer perceive the function assigned to everyone in our community. Things are not working because we believe humans are the product of an accident; meanwhile, a program is embedded inside our DNA. Our existence unfolds according to a set of Information. While our biology unfolds through these programs, our morals want to go against it. Things are so designed for a purpose. Men get angry for a purpose. We don't justify men turning their anger against their wives because that was not the primary motive of rage. Our society is not working because we lack knowledge. Some scholars teach us that life has no meaning; therefore, there is no purpose behind our existence. How wrong they sound! Life has both meaning and purpose and existence as well.

Women don't get angry because they have no enemy to fight against; they are not called to stand in the front. They were designed to stay home with the kids, preparing for the man's return as we lived in the state of nature. The philosophy of Thomas Hobbes helps us understand the phenomenon. As Hobbes stated, life is solitary, poor, nasty, brutish, and short in the state of nature. Anger appeared to be a valuable tool in the physiology of men to solve crises and survive.

Is anger still justified today? No! Why? Our society has evolved. There are no more Vikings to kill and plunder our cities. Is the biology behind men's anger changed? No! Why? We don't know when the next war will break out. Yesterday, the Russians invaded Ukraine, and the Ukrainian soldiers were not women. Men naturally sent women and children to safety and went to the front. Were they going to war with flowers and smiles? No! They need to be angry enough to fight the invaders.

I remember the discussion of Adichie on the set of the show with Trevor Noah[38], where she stated that society must not favor women and children but the weak from both sides. And Noah mockingly portrayed a man from the sinking Titanic claiming to be evacuated because Adichie

---

[38] Trevor Noah received Adichie in the Daily Show to promote her book "Dear Ijeawele." Here is the link: Chimamanda Ngozi Adichie - "Dear Ijeawele" & Raising a Child to Be a Feminist | The Daily Show; https://www.youtube.com/watch?v=czogWQ34X1Y

said the weak should go first. It was a pertinent remark from the comedian; unfortunately, neither the guest nor the host developed the situation and discussed the idea further. Feminists tend to ignore reality, and by doing so, they have made life harder for women. Adichie believed some women are more robust than men, which I agree with, but ceteris paribus, her statement is invalid. You cannot compare a woman in Samoa with a man in Cambodia; in general rule, women are indisposed several days every month. Men don't have menstrual cramps and would never get pregnant for forty weeks at any instant of their lives. Feminists have a laudable ideology, but the scanty information about life and existence is their problem. Life is still a mystery, and we don't know who or what is distributing the cards (I am talking like a philosopher), but one thing is sure: life does not unfold randomly. Nature has its purpose when it designs the male with high testosterone and the female inundated with oxytocin.

An intruder can waltze into our houses at any time to steal; who knows? War in Ukraine is one of the reasons why society keeps teaching boys to be angry, and we praise their aggressivity for training purposes. I want to marry a woman who knows how to fight, especially in this America where everybody is shooting everyone; if my wife knows how to shoot, I will sleep tight. I will understand when she pisses off because I will be sleeping when a thief comes in, and she will go out.

The point here is to redefine the role in the house now that our society has evolved. Our philosophy is clear on that issue; every couple must identify the captain of the house and the second in command. There must always be a pilot and a copilot in the house. I want to be a copilot for a strong woman; there is nothing wrong with it. I can cook rice and know how to take care of the kids. I can change diapers, and I am a great educator. We don't need to send our children to the nursery; after all, don't we make kids for rearing? Why make them and give them to a babysitter? While the copilot prepares himself for an immanence job, the pilot must train herself for a potential invasion if it occurs. Humans haven't changed much; we still struggle to be good. We have police forces to protect us, but our prisons are still full of criminals. For that cause, someone must be trained to be angry because anger helps deal with an aggressor. We appreciate our boys' anger because the male is naturally fit for the job. However, if girls want to take over, society needs to train females. We cannot have two captains in one boat. To charge a phone, we need a plug and a socket. If all are sockets, things will not work correctly. I know we can have socket-socket and plug-plug families today, but notice that these families are not naturally productive. Are they important? Yes, of course! They can make a good correction and educate kids when the plug-socket family fails, and many fail. Several children are abandoned in the street without their parents; these kids need foster care. Thus, plug-plug and socket-socket family types are valuable in our society. Even in these families, roles are still observable. We can never have two captains in one boat; the ship will capsize.

To me, feminists are beating the bush and are not solving any problem; instead, they pour gasoline on the fire. We cannot teach both girls and boys to be angry at the same time. One must be hot, and another cool since both men and women are called to come together to build a family. Society is destroyed because everybody leaves the house in the morning to run after games. Someone must stay home to take care of the kids and cook dinner. It doesn't matter who will stay; the one that goes out must learn self-love and how to be angry because it is nasty outside.

Adichie seemed to experience the same dramatic situation you had encountered in France, but society has improved. The amendment is slow but progressive. She calls herself a happy African feminist who does not hate men, and I am an essentialist feminist who understands women and the society humans have built. I hear both of you, and I grasp your concerns. Your opinion and vision of society will not hold in the future. If you notice closely, many of your statements have already become old-fashioned today. It is an anachronism to continue fighting the battle you fought. Your book "The Second Sex" made waves in the United States, but today, many accounts you stirred up are outdated.

It is true the United States is still lagging, and no woman has yet risen to power in the White House, but the number of independent, self-made millionaires and successful women is staggering. The statistics show more females in colleges than males; the ratio is 60% women against 40% men. I call this progress; yes, American society is on its way to healing.

Life is not fair, and we must not try to make it be. Women, the Jews, and the blacks need to be patient. The white man is waking up but not so fast; indeed, he will mature soon. As Martin Luther King said, I quote:

"Injustice anywhere is a threat to justice everywhere. We are caught in an inescapable network of mutuality, tied in a single garment of destiny. Whatever affects one directly, affects all indirectly[39]."

I hear this great man, and for that cause, I consider Chimamanda's complaints, and I heard yours as well. However, I stopped accusing men as I used to and turning toward women because our children don't fall from the sky; they sojourn in women's wombs. Children spend more time with their mothers than anyone else. So, what do women teach their kids?

On the TV show's platform, Adichie dodged this question and said we live in a world where men are more likely to listen to men. It is a good argument, but feminists often forget that all men have sojourned in a woman's womb; no man on earth falls from the sky. Moreover, children prefer their mothers when they are young; things start changing from the age of reason through adolescence. We have all been children, and our mothers' arms are the safest place to hide and seek comfort. Children spend more time with their mothers than anyone else until modern society has invented the nursery. Even babysitters in our daycare centers are more female than male; thus, the question remains: what do women teach boys?

In your epoch, the biggest problem was the white man and his ideology, but even a woman raises the white man. What did women teach him? Life on earth unfolds in a chain reaction. It

---

[39] Reverend Martin Luther King Jr. penned those words from his cell after his arrest in Birmingham in 1963. The letter was crafted in August 1963 and was titled "Letter from Birmingham Jail." Here is a link to a copy of the letter: https://www.csuchico.edu/iege/_assets/documents/susi-letter-from-birmingham-jail.pdf

takes only one man to establish Christianity in Europe. A single man triggered a revolution and caused the Church's schism, and another man's erroneous trial caused the birth of science. Darwin alone, with his works, upended our communities and created an unprecedented upheaval in our society.

Women have to blame themselves because they raise children. The injustice Adichie suffered in Nigeria was inflicted by men raised by Nigerian women; these men didn't fall from the sky. Here is my question: how do they educate their boys? We need to open our minds to solve problems in our societies. The white man has been the great culprit that foments trouble in our cities, but he did it for a purpose. The entire world has identified him today, and we know about his lies. Now that we know, what shall we do? We keep praying that he recovers his reason, but we cannot wait for the white man to amend everything. We must act, and women are more concerned than anyone else. Adichie puts it well in her book:

"We must raise our daughters differently. We must also raise our sons differently."

I agree, but we cannot educate our children correctly unless we learn to understand life and existence, differentiate between man and woman, and distinguish the demarcation line between dating and marriage. We must comprehend the society we have built and how it is designed to operate.

The problem of feminism is similar to a beautiful woman who wears a sexy dress with cleavage, wearing high heels in the street, and getting mad because people stare at her. What did she think when she went shopping? Sometimes, women love to fool the world. It is time we stop blaming men for everything. The feminist movement must not be a war against men because what happened in the past was done in total ignorance. Religious dogmas blinded men. Notice that women were not the only ones who suffered from men's abuse. Men killed each other as well.

We must see the progress of humanity as a father raising his child. Nature raises us likewise; we receive religion in our childhood. In our adolescence, we got science; today, we are transitioning toward adulthood with spirituality. Your beloved companion labeled it "Humanism," I called it "Essential-humanism."

The next step of our voyage is spiritual enlightenment. The physical enlightenment occurred in Europe during the eighteenth century when philosophers put the brain at the center of human affairs. They focused on the rational mind to grasp nature and study phenomena around them. With spiritual enlightenment, the human heart will be at the center because the spirit resides in the heart; some philosophers call it emotional intelligence.

While religion puts God at the center of human business in the childhood of humanity, the new era will focus on humans; that's what Sartre meant by humanism. In humanity's adulthood, human beings will be set at the center, and the upcoming spiritual enlightenment will be summarized by the seven last laws of the decalogue, also known as the love of humans:

1- "Honor thy father and mother."
2- "Thou shalt not kill."

3- "Thou shalt not commit adultery."

4- "Thou shalt not steal."

5- "Thou shalt not bear false witness against thy neighbor."

6- "Thou shalt not covet thy neighbor's wife."

7- "Thou shalt not covet thy neighbor's goods."

Humans are endowed with empathy, and the only way to express it is by observing these seven laws written inside our chromosomes. The love of humans is the love of God. Notice that the ten commandments are divided into two portions: the love of God and the love of humans. Religious people love God more than humans, but the new recommendation urges them to love one another because nobody has ever seen God. We are made in the image of God, and the only way to prove we love God is to love the humans he created. Saint John stated in one of his epistles that he who loves is born of God and knows God. We must stop fooling ourselves.

Spiritual enlightenment will be a period of a gigantic awakening where society shall display human values openly. People will understand that God seeks to manifest himself in each of us. There will be a back-and-forth communication between God and humans similar to energy and matter. Life incarnates itself in the material universe; it takes a form, moves through, and transforms every object.

For instance, life takes its basic forms as sodium and chloride, which combine to make salt. Plants use sodium chloride to grow and bear fruits. Sheep feed on the tree's leaves, and their meat nourishes humans. After we die, our bodies decompose to feed plants, and the cycle restarts.

Material existence begins with elementary particles that coalesce to build molecules and organic compounds. Living existence springs up to incarnate in objects made of atoms and molecules. After death, the subject returns to the immaterial realm while the object decomposes into its essential components. It is the same God that lives in everything in this universe. "In him, we live and move and have our beings," said Saint Paul.

Another concern of your disciples I would like to talk about is the psychology of man and woman. Feminists will destroy our society if they scoff at human psychology and physiology. We are above animals because we are medium consciousness. We live by instinct, but we also have a rational mind; that's why depression is more common among humans than in other species. Animals don't commit suicide because they don't have a personality; they live by instinct.

Adichie drew attention to one critical point in her book about boys' education concerning money. I would not be tired of opening the eyes of my feminist sisters about this particular question. I don't think a problem could arise with essentialist feminism because we still believe man and woman are complementary entities and have a specific function in society. Your compatriot Nadine de Rothschild is an excellent example, an actress for whom I nourish a great admiration; she is one of the essentialist feminists I know after Plato. Trouble always arises with existentialist feminists, a school of thought in which you are the leader. In this modern society, money has something to do with boys and men. Fighting inequality between man and woman must not lead to another catastrophe. Existentialist feminists tend to forget the physiology of living organisms because they are mostly atheists. We don't have enough resources to prove the existence of God scientifically, but atheists cannot prove materialism either. The existence of functional Information in nature and the body of living organisms connotes the presence of an author. Someone is behind the Information that governs our lives. Life does not unfold randomly. For that cause, man and woman have specific roles to play, and trouble may arise in our communities when we ignore these functions. As I have said, men don't get pregnant.

We must not forget that humans have created a society that follows specific rules. We have established commerce between members of society in such a way that one must pay something to get something. To facilitate the transaction among humans, we invented money. In the olden days, a hunter traded some venison steaks for arrows from the blacksmith. Today, the same hunter must pay cash against the arrows because the blacksmith does not want to eat deer; his family has been eating deer meat all days of the week, and his wife prefers fish this evening. Money facilitates commerce among members of the community. Since men are traditionally designated to put food on the table, they are required to have money in modern society for transactions.

Too many young men don't understand the society we have built; that's why a young student will open fire and murder his comrade girls because he estimates not being attractive. The West and the US are the only places to find preposterous ideas. No matter how beautiful a man is, the gynecologist would want to be paid after consultation. After the accouchement, a man's abs and beautiful face will not cover the medical fee. A girl may crawl at a boy's feet because he is beautiful, but a woman will not do that because she knows adult life is about solving problems. A man's beauty is not required for marriage; his wallet is more needed. Beauty is for dating; a man's ability to solve problems is the main requirement in marriage. The lies we tell our children are the source of tragedy in our communities. We disconnect our youth from reality and are baffled to see them become monsters. What if we start reconnecting the youth with reality? What if we teach them that adulthood is about responsibility?

Of course, our society has evolved, and some women are more successful than men; they understand the game of money better than the male. They take time to discover their talents and work them out to fruition. In that case, the woman can be in charge, and the man assists her in managing the house; there is nothing wrong with it. The pilot is the one who knows how to make money; no one can be a master over a woman's money because he is a man. A function-based role is preferable to a gender-based one. However, there is one law I have discovered in the biology of men: money causes them to be depressed; a man is more likely to be depressed with an empty bank account than a woman. Adichie stresses that we teach boys and girls equally, which is good, but we must not forget to recall to boys that physiology and psychology are playing against them. If the problem is psychological, I believe it is; new knowledge will solve it. But until we reach that point and amend our society, we must train our boys to avoid being depressed. What do you think pushes young boys to believe they are unattractive? They should say they are broke.

In a relationship, women come with a natural value: their womb. A woman does not feel depressed because she lacks money; a man does. In general, women are more likely to be depressed by the state of their relationship, while men tend to sink into depression due to job-related issues. Since work and relationships are the two fundamental pillars of adulthood, the priority seems divided accordingly between men and women. Work connotes an income or money; relationships stand for affection, attention, and intimacy. A man will not be depressed because he lacks attention or affection; he never craves these things. A husband will never complain because his wife fails to compliment him about his physical appearance. Most of his concerns are turned toward work, the source of his income. I often recommend young boys save money when they start working because their minds will be connected to their bank accounts.

The situation seems different for women. A woman cannot wake up and often hear from her partner: "you are beautiful, and I love you," and still be depressed; these words alone would make her day. After a shower, a man does not spend thirty minutes in front of a mirror; women do. They spend a lot of time painting their face; this is the reality for almost all feminine women in modern society. There is a tragedy in our communities because we neglect this reality; our feet are not touching the ground anymore; we live in imagination that does not reflect reality, and the youth is confused.

It is a good point when Adichie proposes we raise our children differently to amend our society in the next hundred years. We are heading toward a paradigm shift, and men and women must be aware of the mechanism underlying the phenomenon. We can teach whatever we want to our kids, but we must make sure our society understands the phenomenon and how it unfolds. Everything is governed by Information that does not come from humans; we are not the author of life. Humans barely understand life and how it develops, so most of our ideologies are absurd. Do we understand life? One of the questions we should ask today is: why is the number of depressions increasing among the population?

Physiology and psychology play crucial roles in our existence; we will run straight into the wall if we don't admit it. Some jobs are more manageable for men to perform than women; I would never ask my wife to hew a tree in the middle of our yard. If we go shopping in town and a dresser accidentally overturns and crushes a kid, I will not send my wife to lift the heavy furniture. Society is evolving, but we must not forget biology; otherwise, everything will be upside down. Essentialist feminism recalls that men and women have some innate functions to play in society. A man does not get pregnant no matter how hard he tries; he has no womb and breasts well-developed to suckle a baby. We must learn to give back to Caesar what is Caesar's and to God what is God's.

We must pay attention to the information we forward to our kids and not raise them by fantasy. The world is upside down right now, and we must be careful to avoid creating another trouble. Radical feminists need to put some water into their wine. I have heard about an experiment some psychologists performed in the last century, and I don't know if the test eventually occurred. Still, the story goes this way: a couple of psychologists built a family and wanted to teach human behaviors to animals. They had a toddler and adopted a baby chimpanzee one of their colleagues offered them after an expedition from Africa. They decided to raise the two infants together, expecting to convert the chimp to behave like a human. It didn't take long before they stopped the experiment because the human infant started acting like a chimp.

I narrate this experiment, which I don't know was an actual occurrence, but my concern here is to warn radical feminists. We must not run faster than we can breathe. It is good to train girls to replace boys, but we must make sure not to turn women into something and men into other things we are unaware of; we must be patient. The time will come, our understanding will expand, and the city will have no criminals. That day, all men will resign from the police department, and we will replace them with women. In book five of "The Republic," Plato believed we should employ women for the same tasks as men; he argued society must give women the same teaching, and we are on it progressively. But until that day entirely comes, we need men to protect the city from violent criminals. Notice that women are not the criminals that roam our city; they are males. Most bandits and offenders are males.

However, women must take some immediate action before this glorious day of men's healing arrives. One of these actions I want our daughters to know is their attire. Women need to consider the way they dress. We live in a free society, but we must comprehend that one's liberty ends where the neighbor's starts. Anarchist feminists are surfing over our society's current crisis to create unnecessary drama. What is the point of exposing one's body parts to strangers? In a free society, we can be naked in our homes and perform for our partners. Once we go outside, our liberty has some limits; it metamorphoses into freedom, a domain where our privilege applies.

When nobody is around, our liberty has no frontier. However, when someone is present, our liberty acquires a border. We must respect our neighbors; otherwise, we will fall into anarchy. Anarchist feminists have difficulty understanding this simple equation. Why wear a dress with high cleavage and complain about men's gaze? It isn't that they wear them to look beautiful. A beautiful thing is made to be appreciated. Women can choose to dress with modesty. They can show their body parts to their partners at home but dress comfortably for work. Women's clothing should not be a big deal in society; you said it earlier: the soft, smooth, and resilient feminine flesh is what arouses sexual desire; do women are aware of it? If they do, why such obstinacy to show off their body parts? I do not care, though.

Women's attire becomes problematic when the dancers complain about the spectators; the dress show organizer does not want anyone to watch her new designs. The mermaid does not want anybody to listen to her beautiful songs. What is the point of showing her beautiful legs in a mini-skirt? Feminists fiercely fight against the objectification of women; they don't want women to be erotic objects for men, yet they wear dresses with high cleavage to show off their breasts. I am sorry to stress the hypocrisy here; someone must say it. As essentialist feminists, we are fair. We have our feet on the ground and are in touch with reality; we tilt neither to the left nor right.

We agree that sexual harassment is sometimes a weapon men use to intimidate women. The human species is selfish by nature, and men are more narcissistic than women. There is no doubt that men are more wicked than women; I have demonstrated that already. However, we must not forget that life is still a mystery, and many phenomena escape our understanding. Do we know what causes men to be wicked? Being wicked is not a good qualification, but some are delighted to promote nefarious ideologies. Religious people say the devil inspires humans, but science can't prove it. Until we prove the devil exists, women must be our first line of defense when mothers raise their boys in due regard to human dignity. I repeat it: boys don't fall from the sky. When parents fail, we have monsters instead of human beings.

If men and women understand the frontier that delimits dating from marital relationships, things can also be different. Men tend to wag their tails everywhere, and society admits males can seduce females. Humans don't date; they marry. Dating is an invention of modern society to increase promiscuity. A woman is not a promiscuous being; otherwise, her psychology will succumb. She was not designed to sleep left and right. Her psychology forbids her, but she can adapt. In this modern society, she is free to be and do whatever she wants. Technically, a married individual cannot have an extramarital affair because he vowed faithfulness to someone. Fortunately, things are changing, and for that cause, our daughters need to know what is at stake for them. They need to grasp the reality of existence and understand its patterns.

Often, feminists, especially anarchist feminists, give a gloomy picture of the reality of women. That's why I toil here to open our daughters' minds. Feminists set you as a model but forget that time has changed. I do not fully understand men's domination in the West and the US; however, I grasp what you have experienced in France, and I could say some of your assertions are polished to grab public attention. Even Adichie was exaggerating; perhaps she focused too much on personal issues. African men might have become horrible to women, but the white man taught them. I grew up in Togo, and I don't think our mothers have complained, as African feminists love to portray it. My father complained about my mother, and he fell into polygamy because my mother was not apt to join him in his business. He desired a European system; unfortunately, my mother didn't have the chance to attend school. My father would desire a woman with business skills but would not tolerate competition. I need to add that he didn't allow my mother to prosper in any business of her choice. He learned from his brother's wife, a successful business owner. That aunt was a leader in the house and canceled my uncle, who was timid by nature. Perhaps my father feared the same thing would happen if my mother prospered independently. African men feared women as modern cities started flourishing in the new republics; I believe the European system has spread to Africa. Today's financial and economic situation demands men to alter course because the world is changing. I noticed we didn't have nice things growing up because our mother was kept broke, and my father's resources alone were limited.

You asked the question, why do women not contest male sovereignty? I would like to enlighten our daughters thereon. Today, feminists tend to portray men as monsters, but the reality is different. Notice that women didn't complain in the past because the productive and reproductive forces were balanced. Men put food on the table and defend the city; women cook meals and provide children for the king's army. Nowadays, the balance between the productive and the reproductive forces is disrupted. There is no more threat to women as it used to be; we have police forces and a strong army to defend our countries. Humanity has evolved, and our behaviors keep improving.

Why is woman the Other? It is not men who forced her to be the second sex; she chose that position in the state of nature. What you labeled the great historical defeat of the female sex had never originated from a battle. Never in the history of humanity have we heard a fight for power between man and woman; the subjugation was consent. Women never saw it as subjugation; anarchist feminists call it so.

Since we exited the state of nature, she never claimed a new place until today. The amendment of our society is slow because men have been conditioned that way, and women as well. Notice that people were not born dictators; they become. If we condition a leader for so long, making him believe he is a demigod, a new habit is formed, and things stay that way. Kings never imposed themselves. Today, people tend to portray royalties as if they imposed their domination upon us. It has never been that way.

In the beginning, the bravest among men stood in the front of the battle, and his courage positioned him to be the "One," and everybody else was behind. Society adulated the intrepid leader and praised him for his courage. The village adored and cherished his children, and they gave them the unique appellation of prince and princess. You will never find the first king who imposed himself on society in human annals. We loved them and conditioned them to that lifestyle.

For instance, in the Bible, Israelites praised King David and loved Solomon, but they rebelled against Roboam, the grandson of David. But before King David, they elected King Saul to lead them in battles. How did David become king? His courage led him to the palace. Anyone could be king in the primitive society of humans. Problems often arose when the danger everyone was running from disappeared. The jealousy and envy of the population awakened when all trouble finally subsided. The situation is similar to that of veterans in our society today. Should we envy veterans that the government treats them well? No! When it was hot, they didn't hide.

While many stayed with their wives and children in their cozy homes, they volunteered themselves and went to the front. They could have been killed, but they survived. He who takes enormous risks must expect a great reward. The same analogy applies to royalties and spreads to men in general. They are enjoying the courage of their ancestors. Who were our parents? They had no courage to step forward. They stayed indoors with their wives. Why should I have to envy a prince today? My ancestors didn't step forward while the post of leadership was vacant. However, princes and princesses must not abuse their privilege. It was a great risk their ancestors took. They would not exist today if the first king were killed in a battle. Princes and princesses today are taking advantage of the seed their ancestors sowed in the past.

Dear Simone, you stand against men today, but your great-grandmother praised their courage and always prayed that men came out during an attack. She begged brave men to come out to defend the village. She loved to be the Other, the second sex. It was a great pleasure for her to be a female. You despised being the Other because things have improved in human society. You don't live in the state of nature, and your life is not continually threatened as it used to be. Even if war broke out, men would step forward and send women and children to safety. What I am saying is not a fabrication, and Ukrainian women could confirm it. When confronted with the Russian aggression, women knew their job was to take children to safety; it was automatic. Nobody came forward to ask why men went to the front, and women ran to safety because it was natural. Are Ukrainian women "the Others?" yes! Are Ukrainian men "the Ones?" yes! Do Ukrainian men make women "the Others?" No! Do women complain? No!

In the jungle, the lion knows his primary role is to defend the territory and protect each member of the pride. It is written in their DNA; there is functional Information inside their chromosomes that dictates such behavior. The female lions hunt and feed the pride; nobody complains about their tasks. Feminists complain because they cannot see the whole picture.

I am not justifying the abuse of men. They have done horrible things to women because religion steps into the matter. The general confusion and ignorance of the topic caused some fellows to err and justify the mistreatment of women. The humiliation of women you have all along mentioned in your book was nothing more than the erroneous interpretation of the work of Charles Darwin. He dethroned religion, which was not doing any good to women. Instead of amending women's situation, social Darwinism poured gasoline on the fire. Women are not alone; the indigenous people outside Europe also suffer and continue to pay the price even today.

However, I can reassure you that the equality between the sexes you have claimed so much will come; it's just a matter of time; men are not monsters. I am a truck driver, and I live in the United States. Fifty years earlier, I was not allowed to circulate freely because I could not go to some places; the law forbade it. Today, I can go everywhere; that alone to me is progress. Things are changing, and we must praise the change, although slow it may seem. As I used to say, life is not fair, and nobody knows what God is doing. If Nature gives someone a penis, he must enjoy it; if it gives someone a vagina, she must also enjoy it or at least give it to someone who can value it. I was born in Africa, so I don't complain. Do I envy a white man? He does not exist; only humans exist, and some have a fairer complexion than others. We have many people with albinism in Africa; if the white man exists, we also have many of them. Nobody quite understands what is going on in this world. Scientists are the least to trust; building planes and launching rockets does not mean they know what is happening. These are programs that are diffused, and anyone who is well-trained could harvest and process them as well. I know how it works.

The false doctrines and ideologies we build to dominate the planet are the problems that plague the world. Today, women rebel because of the humiliation they have been victims of daily from preposterous ideas mediocre men have developed over time through social Darwinism. In the United States, some women refuse to go with men and choose other women's companies because sexuality with men appears humiliating. Is heterosexual frolics humiliating? No! But the domination of mediocre men makes it seem so.

I want to let our daughters know that women voluntarily accepted being the second sex in the past; nobody forced them. They chose it; it had never been imposed on them as anarchist feminists try to sell it to us today. Women nowadays have become victims of misinterpreting data and shoveling radical feminism into our throats. If I were a woman, I would never accept carrying a pregnancy and toiling day and night in warehouses; marriage is teamwork. They are killing women with their claim of equality; we don't need equality between man and woman, but equity-based programs.

The productive and reproductive forces are no longer in equilibrium; women are suffering everywhere in this modern society. They need to set the problem correctly to find a genuine answer. Right now, it's a mess. We have single mothers in every corner of our cities. Our daughters are suffering more than feminists pretend our mothers did in the past. Someone has said the old feminism is dead; it is indeed. The movement does not take into consideration the change occurring in society. Women must not be spectators; they are called to shape our world and have done so since the beginning of history. However, they were not active but passive. So, it is a fallacy when you say the fundamental reason that woman has been consigned to domestic labor and prohibited from shaping the world is her enslavement to the generative function. This statement is not true and stands against historical facts; it is sheer fabrication. Never in history have women been enslaved. They worked alongside men. Let's recapitulate our arguments carefully so our daughters aren't confused.

Dear Madam, I'm afraid to disagree with you when you said the feminine condition was not a continuous process. Men's hegemony and the injustice that followed did not occur overnight. From primitive societies to modern civilizations, women gradually conceded to men's whims. Man's imagination grew bigger with his ambitions, and the woman was always behind to support him. Mothers backed their sons, and sisters praised their brothers' conquest. They admitted man's masculinity without knowing and boosted his ego; step by step, the steamroller was set up. How was it possible that a son could kill his mother? The story reports that Nero assassinated his mother; how did she raise him? The account said she also was a ruthless empress puppeteering behind the scenes. The adage says, like father, like son. Are women passive collaborators of the inhumane behaviors of men? Not all men are evil; why do some become insufferable bullies?

As you pointed out in your book, I could not disagree; men have been horrible to women, but these ones allow it. Everything started during the cognitive revolution, as Yuval Noah Harari labeled it. This era was particular in the development of modern humans. They acquire two frequencies in their creative minds: imagination and intuition. These two new frequencies allowed them to step forward and move out of the animal kingdom.

Humans began to communicate with the unknown realm of the spirit. Their understanding started expanding, and humans commenced to tame nature. In their moves and journeys, they encountered different obstacles. As we have seen already, physiology and psychology allowed men to step forward and stand before danger while women helped find shelters for the kids; it is the same scenario as the war in Ukraine. This phenomenon occurred naturally. While other animals have defense mechanisms like antlers, horns, tusks, fangs, powerful jaws, and claws, humans have nothing to protect themselves against wild animals. They have to rely on their brain, especially their minds that have just acquired two additional frequencies.

Humans used their brains to understand fire and succeeded in taming it. Through the two ways of communication brought in by the frequencies of imagination and intuition, they received visions and new knowledge of nature. They had a glimpse of the anatomy and the physiology of other animals. They knew that a stone thrown at the head of an animal could kill it. They fabricated spears because they understood that animals could be disabled and die if they pierced them. They knew life inside was protected by a boundary fence, and the vital energy would leak out whenever the fence was breached. How did they know all these things? Today, science lets us know that three fundamental elements characterize life on Earth: Functional Information, a boundary fence, and the entangled system Degradation/Synthesis.

While animals defended themselves by instinct, humans forged their defense mechanisms through knowledge. Until that day, the chance was spread evenly between men and women. Women could have seized power, but their physiology and psychology showed they needed men for effective defense and survival. Man never imposed himself;

the situation called upon his courage, and he responded valiantly. Thus, through the cognitive revolution, the man gained ascendancy naturally while the woman took the second position. Her role of caregiver sprang up naturally, while man appeared as the defender of the horde.

When the agricultural revolution occurred, humans finally settled. Here again, women have an equal chance to step forward and possess the lands because the meadow stretched as far as the eye could see. Women didn't leave; they didn't step far away because both man and woman formed an indissociable entity; they were inseparable. They were living a love story, and they settled together and built a community. At that point, nobody claimed the rulership; man didn't step forward to say, "I want to be a king!" It didn't happen that way. Nobody ruled the village until there was an attack. When they settled, everyone was busy with his family; sometimes, they gathered and ate together until a brutal invasion disrupted their peace.

The next attack on the village by another nomadic tribe confirmed to women that they needed men for survival. Willingly, they consecrated themselves to the job they were naturally fit to perform. While men organized the defense of the village through training, women took care of the children and managed the crops. Men became blacksmiths to forge weapons; women became weavers to make fabrics. The division of labor appeared naturally. Men did not appoint women to the domestic tasks; they were naturally fit and happy with that job. They could choose to venture out with men, but the risk was too great. In the forest, people isolate themselves to make their toilets. A woman alone somewhere is too risky. A wandered could jump on her to satisfy his impulses. The risk is too high for a woman to venture far away from the village. She is safe only within the perimeter, where a man could hear her cry and come to the rescue. Remember, even in this modern era, countless cases of rape were reported during the war in Ukraine.

Like the Ukrainian women celebrated the courage of their men and praised their heroism in battles, our mothers saluted man's position. They acknowledged his presence in the tribe; that's why they composed songs for the most courageous among the men of the village, who later became the king. The Bible explicitly reported in 1 Samuel 18:7 the following:

"The women sang as they played and danced, saying, "Saul has slain his thousands, And David his ten thousands."

By raising one man above the crowd, humans established a dynasty without knowing it. As we have said above, humans are creatures of habit. It was women who told men how important they were. Man discovered his value through women's mouths; they made songs and hymns for him. They celebrated his bravery and glorified his courage, and man went to seek more victories for more glory. Women set him up.

The agricultural revolution, which is characterized by a sedentary lifestyle, showed no conquest by man. Women had all the opportunities to step forward if needed, but it had never been necessary. There was no justification for such a thing because women had never seen themselves competing with men; otherwise, they would have left and made a community one hundred miles away from men. The land was available, and people were few on Earth then. Our mothers didn't leave because they understood their position was next to man; in an obligatory symbiotic relationship, the males and the females live in harmony until today. The false claim of feminists will not change history.

Women alterity started with religion. The first drought and the famine that followed made humans question nature. People began to voice their inquietude when the ground shook and opened to swallow their loved ones. And someone had a dream and accused the blacksmith's daughter because she could bleed for seven days. A man who secretively coveted her confirmed she might be guilty because a creature that bleeds out for seven days but still manages to survive must be the incarnation of the devil. The village agreed to sacrifice her to appease the gods. They built an altar and made their offerings. Two days later, the sky sent its rain. The first primitive religion had just been set up, and they offered the gods a virgin every year.

Things got worse when the revealed religions came to the stage. This time, men had written laws against women who kept falling behind as civilization grew. Priests and prophets legislated strict laws against them, and women's menstruations seemed to corroborate men's narrations. Shedding blood was declared impurity, and anyone who touched a woman during her periods was unclean till evening. The law even goes further: one must not sit on whatever she sat on with her issue, let him be declared unclean until the evening. We can read the entire law in Leviticus 15: 19-33 as follows:

"If a woman has a discharge, and the discharge from her body is blood, she shall be set apart seven days; and whoever touches her shall be unclean until evening.

Everything that she lies on during her impurity shall be unclean; also, everything that she sits on shall be unclean. Whoever touches her bed shall wash his clothes and bathe in water, and be unclean until evening. And whoever touches anything that she sat on shall wash his clothes and bathe in water, and be unclean until evening. If anything is on her bed or on anything on which she sits, when he touches it, he shall be unclean until evening. And if any man lies with her at all, so that her impurity is on him, he shall be unclean seven days; and every bed on which he lies shall be unclean.

If a woman has a discharge of blood for many days, other than at the time of her customary impurity, or if it runs beyond her usual time of impurity, all the days of her unclean discharge shall be as the days of her customary impurity. She shall be unclean. Every bed on which she lies all the days of her discharge shall be to her as the bed of her impurity; and whatever she sits on shall be unclean, as the uncleanness of her impurity. Whoever touches those things shall be unclean; he shall wash his clothes and bathe in water, and be unclean until evening.

But if she is cleansed of her discharge, then she shall count for herself seven days, and after that she shall be clean. And on the eighth day she shall take for herself two turtledoves or two young pigeons, and bring them to the priest, to the door of the tabernacle of meeting. Then the priest shall offer the one as a sin offering and the other as a burnt offering, and the priest shall make atonement for her before the Lord for the discharge of her uncleanness.

Thus, you shall separate the children of Israel from their uncleanness, lest they die in their uncleanness when they defile My tabernacle that is among them. This is the law for one who has a discharge, and for him who emits semen and is unclean thereby, and for her who is indisposed because of her customary impurity, and for one who has a discharge, either man or woman, and for him who lies with her who is unclean.'"

It is without comment; the message is clear. This law subjugated the woman and excluded her from the temple service, and she lost de facto any high social function. However, it must also be stressed that these strict laws were not forged against women only. Men had to obey rules for their genital discharge as well. The vaginal discharge from women and the seed of copulation from men were both labeled unclean, but women pay a higher price for their natural disposition. Did God make an error?

As men sought rational explanations for disasters and calamities that could swarm the city, they designated women as the culprit: human society is suffering because the first woman sold humanity; thus was the interpretation offered by religion led by men. It is as absurd as it sounds, but when the wine is drawn, one must drink it. When the Apostle Paul said the head of man is Christ, and the head of the woman is the man, he had just confirmed the series of facts established between man and woman through the ages. Religion came to highlight the division of the sexes that already existed.

The scientific revolution brought the absurdity to its apogee. Scientists came on stage to dethrone religion, and one had to believe these people were more intelligent than religionists, but they were even worse. They used science to nail the stupidity religion started. They used scientific arguments through social Darwinism to display their misogynistic thoughts; some toiled harder than others, but all failed in their attempts because man and woman are inseparable entities. They complete and complement each other; people can prate on this statement to no avail.

Darwin came on stage to pour more gasoline on the fire. His followers erected the white man as the epitome of creation. For them, the white male displayed all the elegance, beauty, strength, and intelligence of the manifestation of existence; life springs as a single cell to reach its pinnacle, the crown of the evolutionary process, as a white man. Unfortunately, they forgot to answer why evolution made living creatures males and females. They were also unable to explain why we cannot call a male dog a man.

From the enlightenment era to the Darwinian revolution, dumb things have been said about women. For Arthur Schopenhauer's misogyny, I could understand him because he got into trouble with a woman who sued him and lived on his expenses for the rest of her life. The bitterness of the German philosopher toward women is graspable; he hated women for a purpose. In his essay "On Women," he explicitly treated women as the "sexus sequior," or the second sex, an article you had probably read, and whence I believe you drew the title of your book, "The Second Sex." I pray that you may excuse his harsh words toward women.

Dear Simone, you have painted a gloomy tableau, somehow true, of the existence of women. However, your account has some embellishments to gaslight women. It is an exaggeration to tell our daughters that men have enslaved women; we must avoid such rhetoric at all costs. The relationship between man and woman has always been lovely, although things often do not work as expected by women. I blame the failure of relationships upon women themselves because they don't understand the constitution of man. That's why I moil day and night to instruct our daughters on the reality of existence on planet Earth. While things appear depressing in the marital house, women have a beautiful story to tell in business and public affairs.

Here are some great achievements of women who defy all odds to climb the social chessboard and play an important role on the international scene: Angela Merkel, Hilary Clinton, Michelle Obama, Theresa May, Melinda Gates, Christine Lagarde, Dilma Rousseff, Condoleezza Rice, Ellen Johnson Sirleaf to mention only a few. There are an unprecedented number of self-made multi-millionaire women in America, and the number keeps growing: Oprah Winfrey, Rihanna, Sheryl Sandberg, Beyoncé, Kim Kardashian, Kylie Jenner, Selena Gomez, Lady Gaga, Taylor Swift, and many others.

Some women have understood that all humans have been equipped with talents embedded in their chromosomes. They know men don't distribute gifts; God does. Instead of sitting down and whining, many modern women take their fate into their own hands. Women start making their way because they understand the illusion of men's domination. My friend Ramshi from India said women contribute to men's behavior. Of course, they do; boys don't fall from the sky.

The environment has been made safe enough for women to thrive. Adele, Rihanna, Lady Gaga, Selena Gomez,

Ariana Grande, Angelina Jolie, Madonna, and many other singers and actresses understand that talents speak louder. And those who trained their brain are making a high impact in science: Francoise Barre-Sinoussi, Elizabeth Blackburn, Jocelyn Bell Burnell, Chien-Shiung Wu, Jennifer Doudna, Emmanuelle Charpentier, and the list goes on. Our daughters need to understand there are keys that unlock human existence, and it is the individual's responsibility to find those keys. Ladies who want to make it successfully in life must toil to find these keys.

Women can be pilots of the house. Erstwhile, society conferred them the unique role of copilots. When the environment was not safe enough, society confined them to the house for their own protection. Today, we have a strong army and police forces in place, and women can now go out and come as they please. A lot of work needs to be done for their adventure at night, but they are safe to carry on any business they want in the daytime. A woman does not depend on the man anymore. The statistics show there are more college graduate females than males. Our daughters have much to rejoice as time has changed. The ball is in their court. Adichie provides a manifesto with fifteen suggestions to raise Chizalum. It all comes down to parents; mothers are in the spotlight. How will they educate their children to respond to the new environment? Lady Gaga, Rihanna, Adele, Serena Williams, Selena Gomez, and Oprah Winfrey were not princesses. They didn't come from a royal family; they made it from scratch. From our previous narration, where the human infant started acting like a chimp, our daughters would resemble these ladies when they learned something from them. Everything comes down to education. Today, we know that nurture always prevails over nature. I do not want to hide these two concepts from our daughters. It has been a long-standing debate among scientists after the British sociologist coined the term in social Darwinism.

Scientists in those days had no cognizance of functional Information in our bodies; they believed in materialism, thinking life emerged on Earth through chemical reactions. How wrong they were; the proponents of such a theory would struggle to stand in a public debate in front of a knowledgeable audience today. When Anthony Flew noticed the information-bearing properties of the cells of our organs, he changed his position; it is called fair play. He did not become a pastor or a clergyman; he became a reasonable observer, thus, a scientist.

Nature stands for genetics in the nature versus nurture concept, while nurture represents the environment or education. One can be genetically equipped and mess it up; the individual will not become an engineer because his father was a famous inventor. Genes will not work until you work. It is the desire of the individual and his character, forged by the environment, that helps achieve success. Thomas Edison, the most prolific inventor in American history, had several of his children become inventors because they followed his footsteps; carrying the genes is not enough; one must work. It gives some advantages, though, but nurture always prevails. Serena and Venus Williams didn't become champions by sleeping; they practiced and perfected whatever genetics their father might have started editing in his DNA. Nurture is always superior to nature; education steps forward birth conditions. An adage attributed to the Greek philosopher Aristotle said: "Give me a child until he is seven, and I will show you the man." And he proved his point in the life of his pupil Alexander the Great. He made the boy conquer the world.

Our daughters must understand that nurture is always preferred to nature. Today, people are born with disabilities, yet they end up being celebrities; they win medals and awards in international competitions and games. Here is proof our society has changed for the better, and the amendment continues. There are no more excuses for women to play the victim cards; the same applies to other minority groups as well.

I read somewhere the fantastic story of a little girl who was boarding a plane with her mom. The pilot spotted the young girl at the aircraft entrance and said to her: "do you know that you could be a flight attendant when you grow up?" The seven-year-old girl responded boldly to her mother's astonishment and everybody boarding the plane: "I could also own the plane." Here is the mindset we want to communicate to our daughters: a winner mentality. And this would never be possible unless we take away the old feminist mentality, which is now destructive to women. The only thing we ask society is to move all obstacles in the pathway of our children. We don't ask for equality because it cannot be; we cannot compare two incomparable things. There is no way to compare a rotor and a stator; both have a specific role to play. They keep their meaning and significance only when they stay together; separately, they are useless.

Feminists call your book their Bible; Adichie wants to add to it. I have nothing against it, but the time has come for the young generation to escape the victim mentality and embrace the opportunity offered. The ray of light we perceive is a rising Sun instead of a setting one; we must raise our children to see the world differently now that our daughters know how men and women are so designed and why both behave the way they do. The new knowledge is their asset.

The Nigerian feminist recalled one experience in her "Feminist Manifesto" that caught my attention. She narrated one of her experiences where she was stuck in a roomful of young women, and all these ladies had to say revolved around men. These young ladies discussed men's wrongdoing, counting what men had done to them. One evoked how her man lied and cheated on her, and another gossiped about the wedding the man promised but later disappeared.

Adichie believed a roomful of men would not be a conversation full of misery and lamentation; if men have to confabulate about women, they often speak about their conquest. And you seemed to confirm her point of view in chapter 14 of the second volume when you said, I quote:

"It is far more rare to hear a woman talk good-naturedly about a former lover than a man about his mistresses."

The relationship between man and woman must not be mysterious; things are not working correctly because both men and women have scanty information about each other. Since women stand at the passive end of the manifestation of the Energy (life), our daughters must take responsibility for themselves. Nature has imposed on them unfairly; thus, they must reinvent themselves and stop being victims. The victim mindset is what I want to avoid for our daughters; the more they know about the constitution of man and the society we have built, the better they will navigate the meanders. Why do women have to focus on marriage and make their lives revolve around it? The Nigeria feminist questioned. She pointed the finger at the men's domination, which I do not disagree with, but did this phenomenon exist in Africa? Men's dominance explains feminism in Europe, but what about Africa? My main concern here is to separate the two continents, although they have been strongly connected these last centuries. Does feminism have any significance in Africa? I understand what women have endured in the West and the US; do the sub-Saharan African women share the same reality?

As we know today, girls' general desire to marry has been contingent on the old Western and Judeo-Christian rules that only respect and consider married women. In the olden patriarchal system in Europe, a woman was nothing unless tied to a man. We have many examples in the Bible, both the Old and New Testaments because the scriptures influenced European culture tremendously. Since the Frankish king, Clovis, European habits and customs were traceable to the Bible. The three monotheistic religions that emerged in the Middle East always put women under tutelage, which was not the case in Africa until Islam spread in the Middle Ages.

Africa was not fundamentally patriarchal. Patriarchy is a foreign ideology that develops over time, but still, it is a superficial phenomenon; it is not ingrained in our culture. While erstwhile marriages might put the European woman in a vassalage condition, the situation was quite different in Africa; bonding with a man had never been perceived as conjugal shackles for the simple reason that the African man sought to dominate nobody. Physical and economic dominations were truly deep-rooted in European society and are still perceptible today. Africans had never nourished great economic endeavors until the Europeans came. Our caste system had no warlords; there were no Knights and Lords holding serfs and slaves as it were in Europe because the forest fed everybody. Our society was based on subsistence, while the West had been, for so long, economically adventurous.

History taught us how mercantilism evolved in Europe with the advent of the caravels; these small but fast-moving Spanish and Portuguese sailing vessels made the era of exploration possible. While the Europeans engaged in global trade, Africa was still thriving in a subsistence economy. Thus, women were in control of this particular type of economy in Africa, providing another reason the continent did not go patriarchal. Women often dominate local commerce and activities in Africa, centered around subsistence.

Meanwhile, in Europe, the patriarchal organization was a heritage of the feudal system with the support of religious authorities. The mercantilism era came to exacerbate the situation this time, adding economic domination to the social cleavage and caste system in vogue formerly. Voyages at sea were dangerous enterprises; even if these adventures were offered to women, they would not take the bait because women don't crave danger; their psychology forbids it. A woman is not designed as a risk-taker because she incarnates immanence; she is the essence of love and the guardian of life. Intrepid explorers were men, and they responded to the challenge. I recall that men did not block women from going to sea; the ocean was open, and only those capable of braving the storm were worthy to stand.

As it occurred during the cognitive and agricultural revolution, once again, women gave up and encouraged their husbands, brothers, fathers, and sons to venture out and challenge the unknown. Nobody ever stopped women from thriving; the risk was too high, and women were not physiologically and psychologically equipped for the challenge. Thus, the situation was similar to what happened during the previous revolutions; I recall it briefly.

Men and women evolved equally during the cognitive revolution seventy thousand years ago; there is a slight difference between men's and women's brains. The difference lies in the way the two individuals perceive the world. As I have said already, women have a beautiful and harmonious Representation of the world, while men see chaos and find their happiness in the challenge in front of them. Men and women evolve by transcendence and immanence, but the first attribute dominates in men while women conserve the second as a fundamental property. Thus, women allowed men to take the front line in their migration. And women praised their courage and composed songs to celebrate the bravest of the men. The scenario was still the same during the agricultural revolution until the first royalties came to be. Men's hegemony sprang gradually and naturally; nothing had been forced, and nobody was kept behind. Women themselves never complained about the situation; the war in Ukraine is another fresh piece of evidence.

By the time the mercantilism era opened, women were economically broke to join the adventure, and dangers were still standing in their way. The Church also had sapped their morale and convinced them of their alterity; even if women were willing to invest, they lacked funding and firmly believed in the role the Church had assigned to them. Religious authority convinced women and made them think they were the cause of the downfall of humanity, and many women lived their lives in repentance. Almost all traditions teach the same thing; all three monotheistic religions agree that a woman caused the fall of humanity. The Greeks also believed suffering spread into the world at the hands of Pandora; this young and beautiful lady with a gnawing curiosity opened the box her husband forbade her to open. She unleashed evil, curses, and all unimaginable disasters one could ever think upon humanity. The mental prison men forged for women worked well, and the chain of abuse continued until the scientific revolution. Science opened women's minds to their own condition, and both you and Adichie stand to defend the cause of women. I am in this battle today because of the exaggeration you put into your narrations to undermine and weaken our daughters' minds. Both of you point the finger at the same abuse that has a different genesis.

In Africa, the problem between man and woman was set up differently. I understand both of you; your complaints might be justified, but Adichie's remarks give me some urticaria; it is an illusion that men have impeded women's development to dominate them in Africa. African people were not adventurous, and women dominated the local commerce; I said it already. In the olden days, the Arab traders brought their goods through the trans-Saharan trade, and women ensured their distribution locally. In Africa, women have always dominated the trade, and it is still visible today: there are more women in Africa's local market than men. Anyone could visit the continent and confirm this statement. African culture assigns the role of bargaining and exchanging to the females; since the economy has always been subsistence, a conflict between a man and woman is a sheer fallacy. The Nana Benz of Togo is one blatant proof of my assertion. These are wealthy businesswomen who dominated Lomé's Great Market in the Republic's early days. In those days, they used to roll in Mercedes Benz (hence the nickname Nana Benz; Nana means lady) and supply their luxurious cars to the nascent government when outstanding events occurred. Nana Benz's luxurious vehicles helped the government transport the guests during international conferences and summits. In comparison, when the European women were under tutelage in the nascent stage of their nations, these African women had more liberty and power; they were very successful as their country launched after independence in the aftermath of World War Two.

Men have never dominated women in Africa; the pseudo-domination occurred with European colonization. On the continent, everybody knows children belong to women. Contrary to Europe, where boys belonged to their fathers, all children sit and eat with their mothers in Africa. Children also share their mother's room[40]; the husband often has an independent bedroom, inviting their wives by turns.

---

[40] In chapter 5 of his book "L'enfant Noir", Camara Laye described the habits and customs of a typical African family. The author portrayed the role of the African woman within the family.

African men mainly were polygamous, and women divided the weeks between them; the one who cooked slept with the man.

I grew up in a polygamous family, and our mothers used to take turns. The first wife often has authority, but the husband prefers the lady of the last marriage; he enjoys her presence the most, but all women share the weeks equally. Although my father was dominant, he always fought to involve his wives in his business; I could agree with him on that fact. Later, as we grew up, he complained to us and accused my mother of making his plan derail. He had always longed for the European model of household: a husband, a wife, and two or three children. My father didn't want the African traditional family system in the first place, and I understood when I studied his hard work ethic.

There is another crucial argument against the feminist movement in Africa that our daughters must not ignore: it is sexuality. Sex is one fundamental parameter Western women use as an indirect alibi to revolt against men; one aspect of this revolt is manifested by lesbianism, as you described it well in "The Second Sex." Here also, Africa and Europe part ways. After escaping the control of the church, the European men shattered the shackles religious authorities had put on their sexuality. As you exposed the situation in chapter 8 of the book's second volume, "many men demand fantasies from the woman. Marie Therese complained that the French have an insatiable imagination." In Africa, people didn't have sex for pleasure until now. Our ancestors had never done sex as a pleasurable activity, and one reason was their tendency to cut women's clitoris. Sex had always been a way of procreation until the Europeans came, and I believe Adichie could confirm my assertion.

For instance, if a young woman in the neighborhood spotted a single and able man carrying a plate to buy food in the street, she would willingly offer her service; this is a reality in Africa. Things might be changing today, but not so fast. When I was back from France, I still remember being mocked and called all kinds of names because I remained single, whereas I was undergoing a particular program. The African society does not understand why a man with a job capable of taking care of a family could remain single. The vision is the opposite in the West and the US, where people value individual freedom and have enough room to commit themselves to a cause other than marriage. My childhood friends told me nobody could carry out scientific research without funding; I did mine without financial assistance or high-tech equipment; this is a parenthesis.

Marriages in Africa are about mutual services men and women provide each other. The woman brings her womb, and the man offers shelter and protection. As one passage of your book says, referring to women, "Marriage is intended to deny her a man's liberty." The situation is a tad different as African society has its own way of taking women's liberty. I discovered this through investigations I carried out years ago when I returned from France. I will be pleased to share this finding with you, but you have to keep it to yourself because African people will not appreciate that I disclose their secrets. Bear with me that infidelity was rare in Africa because the population didn't practice sex for pleasure (things have changed now).

Moreover, African people believed in Voodoo; at least, Voodoo was a popular belief that permeated the erstwhile society, and the fear of falling under a spell or curse was ubiquitous. For instance, most houses built before 1991 in Togo had at least a talisman. The year 1991 was the collapse of the Soviet block and the advent of Democracy in Africa, which brought alongside the American Evangelical Church. The spread of the Gospel changed people's behavior and mindset, but Voodoo dominated their thinking before then.

Every husband built his house with a talisman; some had two, depending on the ethnic group. People buried the first fetish at the sill of the gate; the second often was buried in the middle of the house. The first one was called "Déma," which means "the constitution of the house." The second was labeled "Apéli or Apélété," which translates as "The one that holds the house stand." The man who built the house made his vow and spoke all his desires to the spiritual entity supposed to dwell in these fetishes. Then he made a bloody sacrifice. Often, they killed domestic fowl, the male animal, for the talisman at the gate, and the fetish in the middle of the house received the blood of the female animal. African people are aware of such sacrifices; thus, people did not err to ogle at their neighbor's wives. Moreover, men were polygamous, eliminating the need for such behavior.

The idea behind the "Déma" is that everyone coming into the house must step over it since it is buried across the gate sill. The husband informs all her wives about the constitution of his home; adultery is always part of these laws. They would agree and vow allegiance to the man; she who violates it and commits adultery (the technical name is "went astray") will have her conscience defiled as she has given her words and taken the oath. It was commonly believed that the spirit behind the talismans would act and punish the violator; thus, women often feared for their lives. Here is another parenthesis to say Africa and Europe have different realities.

As I am about to close this section, frankly speaking, Afro-feminism does not mean anything because African society is not patriarchal as it used to be in Europe; the quotidian of the individuals is also different. The patriarchy penetrated the African continent through foreign cultures. We have significant evidence of this statement in the Bible, where the Queen of Sheba (current Ethiopia) visited Solomon, the king of Israel. In those days in Israel, women were not authorized to reign over the country because the law forbade them to lead men. While women were living in alterity in Israel, African women thrived because the Kingdom of Sheba had a queen.

Feminism is a European problem because of the way European society was structured. Africa and Europe didn't experience the same challenges. The climate played a critical role against the Europeans; the scarcity of food and harsh weather caused the male individual in Europe to develop a certain aggressivity, which was irrelevant in erstwhile society in Africa. People in the jungle lived in relative harmony, and conflicts were not as frequent as they used to be in places where adversity is quotidian, like in Europe.

Africans began facing severe challenges when slave trades started developing. The need for strong men to establish a defense and protect cities and villages emerged, but the conversion to Islam quickly offered protection against raiders. The next threat came later from the European explorers who started raiding in the sixteenth century of this common era, capturing able individuals for slave trades as the discovery of the American continent changed things radically.

Before the Europeans got in touch with the continent, they were already rooted in patriarchy. The destruction of Jerusalem and the Israelites' exodus brought Jewish culture into Europe, while Christianity became Rome's national religion. The Hebrew tradition profoundly influenced the Europeans, who evolved in the same ideology and subjugated women.

When the continent's colonization began in the nineteenth century, the European culture had been imposed on the Africans, and gradually, the continent adopted a system dominated by the patriarchy. Even today, the patriarchal system appears on paper, but the reality is different because African people don't have an ideology of domination. Nobody in Africa sees anything to conquer, less dominate a human being. A woman who feels oppressed in Africa is probably exaggerating; how can a man who has three or five wives force himself upon one who is unavailable? Anyone who studies the history of Africa can notice that nothing justifies the feminist movement; European ideologies, especially social Darwinism, brought discrimination into the continent. They divided African people to conquer them; the genocide in Rwanda is one sequel of European manipulation.

Afro-feminists are individuals who flourish in imagination. Afro-feminism is more about mirage than reality. I understand the fight feminists make in the West and the US; their activism is justified. Women in some traditional Arab countries and places with Islamic traditions might also need feminist fighters because the three monotheistic religions are fundamentally patriarchal. Still, feminism combat in sub-Sahara Africa is a waste of time and energy. Feminism advocates for women's rights in places where those rights were threatened or taken away; Africa does not fully enter that definition. Perhaps African feminists expect to solve the problem of female genital mutilation or child marriage; in that case, their activities do not fit into the original definition of feminism. Genital mutilation and child marriage are all religion-based ideologies. While male circumcision seems justified from a religious point of view, female excision is a misinterpretation of the ancient texts.

I am concerned by Adichie's position, and I am not against her, though. I comprehend the cry of African feminists, but I am calling their attention to the fact that Africa has its anteriority, and people never complained until the Europeans came. Our reality is different, and Afrofeminists must avoid sowing confusion in Africa because we have other fish to fry. We are allowed to weep when our friend loses a child, but grabbing the dead body to dig a tomb in our house to bury the deceased is unacceptable. African feminists can back up their friends in the West and the US and support them in their fight, but there is no need to open a battlefield in Africa.

Dear Madame de Beauvoir, I get your point because the European man is a conqueror by nature; his mentality is different from that of the African man. This statement is a fact and can still be checked today. The African man is not raised with the idea of scarcity, lack, and urgency. He feels no need to conquer or dominate anyone; any resemblance is a photocopy of the old European lifestyle, which is now obsolete. Something caused the feminist movement to emerge in Europe; Africa has no such cause. The following passage from the first chapter of the last part of the first volume of your book summarizes everything:

"Conquering is more fascinating than rescuing or giving. The average Western male's idea is a woman who freely submits to his domination, who does not accept his ideas without some discussion, but who yields to his reasoning, who intelligently resists but yields in the end."

Conclusion

Dear Madame de Beauvoir, your opinion and vision of human society no longer hold. You have been a great captain leading women against men, but the war is over; radical feminism is an anachronism today. One is born woman, and a woman is a womb. Yes, woman is our mother, sister, and daughter; through a new perspective, she can integrate and flourish in a society dominated by men. Our daughters could never win in this battle unless they embrace their nature which is designed to thrive in the world of immanence. She is a queen in her universe and invites the man to her palace. It is an error to claim equality because man and woman are two incomparable entities; there is no need to destroy anything because none is inferior or superior. Radical feminists want to drive all women out of the universe of immanence, but they are not God and cannot decide for everybody. Not all women are under hormones, and some want to prosper in their natural environment. Some women enjoy their womanhood and desire to take advantage of their motherhood, which has more meaning next to man. Both man and woman make sense when they stay together; they complete and complement each other and manifest the same essential needs of the other. Therefore, human society needs an equity-based program instead of the equality-based plans we have deployed since then, which unfortunately are not working. Menstruation and pregnancy are two good reasons to discard an equality-based plan; these are conditions that weigh women down, and no matter how strong a woman can be, some menses can confine her to bed.

Man invented woman because she allowed it, but things could change for our daughters if they understand the situation and the traps men have set up. A confrontation between man and woman is what our daughters must avoid at all costs. For that cause, young girls must obliterate the victim mentality radical feminism has been feeding our sisters for eons. Our daughters must think differently and accept nature's imposition by confining woman to immanence. Being in the state of immanence is not a synonym for inferiority, and teaching our daughters to encroach on the territory of transcendence is working against one's own nature. Life is not fair, and we must not seek it to be; existence on planet Earth only lasts 120 years. By embracing her nature, the woman will find peace, harmony, and equilibrium to thrive better in her universe, which has never been separated from man's world. Today, we know a male is a man and a woman inside; a female as well, meaning both entities are indissociable. Man and woman are essential beings; in the erstwhile society, we distinguished them as the "One" and the "Other." If we look intelligently, there is only "one house" in this modern society; the middle wall of partition between man and woman has crumbled, and only the sequel of the division persists. If our daughters don't believe it, they will not be established. The conflict will last as long as men and women don't understand they are in an obligatory symbiotic relationship.

Our society has highly metamorphosed; a lot of progress has been made and continues to be made. It's time to bury the hatchet. You lived in a troubled period of human history between two great wars, and these moments did not sum up the human journey. Life is a two-person journey; that's the ultimate thing I have learned about it. Indeed, life is a journey, but some people focus too much on details that they miss the whole thing. Under a microscope, life is not fair, but it is a worth-living journey when we apprehend existence as a whole. And because Nature has imposed women unfairly, we must toil to amend society by taking some corrective measures. Men of goodwill are ready to assist women in this battle because they know that the male individuals are more favored than the females. Therefore, equity-based plans are preferred over equality-based programs; there could never be a competition between man and woman. Radical feminism has led women onto a dangerous terrain. Humans are creatures of love, equipped with reason and judgment. We are endowed with empathy; for that cause, we desire to amend society and allow women a comfortable and safe ride in life's journey.

Sometimes, your exaggerated account of the situation is appalling, dear ma'am. I do not exclude man's domination over women. Indeed, women have suffered injustice from men, and you nail it in your book, but I have to clarify to our daughters that man has never conquered woman. He has never set himself as master over women; events unfold naturally. The world has always belonged to men because women give it to them. It was not the man who made woman the Other; she willingly set herself behind to support and assist man. All these events happened because both entities carried functional Information in their chromosomes. Man has always been a woman's baby, and she cherished him in his endeavor. She encouraged his expeditions and praised his courage. A woman gives birth to the man; she educates him before marrying him. So, the question arises: how does she educate him?

In the beginning, our planet was a no-man's-land until strong men claimed it. Women were present at the time, and their number equaled men. That's proof there has never been a conflict between man and woman. Both have always worked together as a team; it is a love story between them, which unfortunately does not end well in most cases. Man has never sought to dominate woman as feminists pretend. Man and woman have an obligatory symbiotic relationship, which can still be proved today. Often, people say a woman, without her, man is nothing. And they are not wrong because the human species will go extinct after three generations when women come missing suddenly. Women hold a strategic position in the puzzle of life.

Women's claim to be recognized as existents just like men is justified, but our daughters need to know that men have never created a feminine domain to lock up women. For that cause, we toil day and night to set up a program to open their minds to the joint partnership between man and woman. Early in the age of consciousness, young girls must do the self-awareness operation before leaving high school. They have two fundamental decisions to make. First, they choose one pool between celibacy and partnership. Second, they decide whether to preserve their body or enter reproduction.

Our girls must understand that adulthood is exclusively challenging, and time plays against them. The clock is ticking for those who choose to build a family and procreate, and they must not waste their time with boys and immature men. Seven steps lead to a healthy and happy relationship. It starts with a flirt. Then the two individuals become friends to learn from each other. As communication naturally flows between them, they upgrade to good friends where honesty, integrity, and loyalty allow both to become intimate. From lovers, they become good lovers. When our daughters discover kindness, empathy, and flexibility as dominant qualities in the suitor, they can safely tie the knot to become parents. The pilot of the house must be able to put food on the table; productivity and time management are the quintessential ingredients to having a stable home. To be good parents, fulfill their jobs, and pay their debt toward society, parents must raise able adults to carry on the purpose of life and contribute to the community's growth.

It is imperative our daughters distinguish life from its manifestation. They must understand the constitution of man to differentiate him from woman to set the demarcation line between dating and marital relationships. Men crave sex, while women long for intimacy. Sex and intimacy are two different things; one can have sex without being intimate. As you demonstrate, men thrive by transcendence while women live by immanence. Our daughters will be miserable if they go against their physiology and psychology. Depression is creating havoc among women because they chronically lack attention and affection from their partners; they operate against their biology, and many don't grasp the trend of this modern society. Essentialist feminism comes to expand their understanding of the true nature of human beings and the reality of the society we have built. It's time to exchange the victim mentality for a winning attitude. A novel mindset is a new destiny.

Dear Madame de Beauvoir, should we all be feminists? I think we are already; we are all born essentialist feminists fighting against dangerous ideologies and doctrines of anarchist feminists. I believe human society is evolving, and our daughters need to increase their understanding of man and the society he has built. Women perish because they think a man is like a woman. Man's psychology is different, and society has managed to set up a judiciary system to put a bridle on his appetite. A government system arises in our cities to put a brake on man's desire and limit his liberty to protect women. Now, he has a well-defined domain to express his freedom as women wake up. No crime will go unpunished, but before that, women must do their parts; they must play their roles in the first place. They cannot fully step into their functions if they ignore what I have shared with you. Mediocre men are afraid of women; a good reason our daughters need to open their eyes and proceed carefully without falling into men's traps. The new knowledge is their asset.

Our daughters must understand these things to stop warring against men; there has never been a conflict between the two entities. Women must hold their ground and thrive in their universe; the world has evolved. People who don't have peace of mind are mad at their entourage and often go to war with the rest of the world. Women are mad today not because men are evil; they don't understand modern society. They don't grasp the society humans have built; both men and women create the modern society together. Men didn't do it without women; sisters supported their brothers; wives assisted their husbands; queens backed their kings, and empresses agreed with the program of their emperors.

Feminism and other false doctrines are time-related phenomena and will disappear with time. Thomas Edison, Rudyard Kipling, and Theodore Roosevelt debunked the supremacy of the Europeans. They prove one can be born outside of Europe and achieve great things. Joe Louis and Jesse Owen proved to Hitler that nothing exists as a superior race. Oprah Winfrey, Rihanna, Lady Gaga, Adele, Taylor Swift, Beyoncé, Selena Gomez, J.K. Rowling, Angela Merkel, Ellen Johnson Sirleaf, Elizabeth Blackburn, and Serena Williams prove that men's domination is an illusion in the mind of society. These women don't fall from the sky; they eat the same food, drink the same milk as our daughters, and send a strong message outside to encourage young ladies. A woman who can extirpate the victim mindset from her thinking system will achieve the same result; she who can separate life from existence and differentiate between man and woman will have a similar ending. A lady who distinguishes dating from a marital relationship will avoid emotional catastrophe. Any young girl who can escape the whims of her emotions can delve inside her chromosomes to find her God given gift; that's where the journey starts. She can break away from the patriarchal system; with courage and hard work, she can boldly state like Shonda Rhimes: "I don't need a man."

An Important Note From the Author

I don't know how to explain to some folks that I am not religious. Jesus was not a religious guy; God Himself is not religious. If you want to be a religious fellow, that's fine, but remember, I am not and will never be. I spent my entire life investigating humans and the manifestation of life on Earth. Religious people don't carry out research; scientists do. Religious people are not free, but God promotes freedom, which Jesus delivers to humans through his teachings. In his letter to the Galatians, Paul said it well: law and Grace cannot coexist.

Always remember: I failed to be a religious dude. Now, I am a Christian philosopher and a theoretical scientist. I do not envy religious people; they must not forget to enjoy their status. Thanks

"I wouldn't have spoken if they hadn't been killing each other."

References

Adichie, C. (2015) "We Should All Be Feminists," Anchor Books

Adichie, C. (2018) "Dear Ijeawele, or A Feminist Manifesto in Fifteen Suggestions," Anchor

Albert, P. (2015) "Why is depression more prevalent in women?" Journal of Psychiatry and Neuroscience

Alexander, E (2012) "Proof of Heaven: A Neurosurgeon's Journey into the Afterlife," Simon & Schuster

Aristotle, (1999) "Politics," Translated by Benjamin Jowett; Batoche Book-Kitchener

Bouakira, A. and De Rothschild, N. (2009) "Réussir l'éducation de nos enfants," Lausanne- Favre

Camara, L. (1953) "L'Enfant Noir," Plon

Chapman, G. (2015) "The 5 Love Languages: The Secret to Love that Lasts," Northfield Publishing

Darwin, C. (1859) "On the Origin of Species"

De Beauvoir, S. (2010) "The Second Sex," Translated by Constance Borde and Sheila Malovany Chevallier, A Knopf; New York

De Beauvoir, S. (1956) "The Second Sex," Translated by H. M. Parshley; Johnatan Cape-London

De Beauvoir, S. (1949) "Le Deuxième Sexe," Volume I; Gallimard-Paris

De Gouges, O. (1791) "Déclaration des Droits de la Femme et de la Citoyenne"

De Rothschild, N. (2001) "L'Amour est affaire de femmes, " Robert Laffont

Descartes, Rene (1637) "Discourse on the Method of Rightly Conducting One's Reason and of Seeking Truth in the Sciences" Part II and Part V.

Descartes, Rene (1641) "Meditation on First Philosophy," Meditation VI.

Chopra, D. (2019) "Metahuman: Unleashing Your Infinite Potential." Harmony Books.

Erasmus, D. (1936) "The Education of a Christian Prince," New York W.W. Norton

Foucault, M. (1978) "The History of Sexuality," English translation copyright by Random House Inc

Freud, S. (1927) "The Ego and the Id" English Translation, London, Hogarth Press and Institute of Psychoanalysis

Geddes, D. and Kinsey, A. (1955) "An Analysis of the Kinsey Reports on Sexual Behavior in the Human Male and Female," New American Library of World Literature: New York

Harari, Y. (2015) "Sapiens: A Brief History of Humankind" Harper

Harari, Y. (2017) "Homo Deus: A Brief History of Tomorrow," Harper

Hobbes, T. (1651) "Leviathan: or the Matter, Form, and Power of a Common-Wealth, Ecclesiasticall and Civil," Green Dragon-London

Hughes, J. (2004) "The Role of Happiness in Kant's Ethics," aporia.byu.cdu

Kaku, M. (2015) "The Future of the Mind: The Scientific Quest to Understand, Enhance, and Empower the Mind," Anchor

Kant, E. (1998) "Groundwork of the Metaphysics of Moral" Cambridge University Press (Page 69-70)

Kant, E. (1784) "What is Enlightenment?"

Kinsey, A., Pomeroy, W., Martin, C. and Gebhard, P. (1953) "Sexual Behavior in the Human Female," W.B. Saunders

Lemaitre, G. (1927) «Un Univers homogène de masse constante et de rayon croissant rendant compte de la vitesse radiale des nébuleuses extragalactiques" Annales de la Societe Scientifique de Bruxelles.

Lemaitre, G. (1950) "The Primeval Atom"

Meyer, S. (2009) "Signature in the Cell: DNA and the Evidence for Intelligent Design" Harper One

Ojeda, A. (2005) "Male/female roles," Greenhaven Press, San Diego-California

Ohsumi Y. (2016) "Molecular Mechanisms of Autophagy in Yeast" Nobel Lecture, December 7, 2016, Tokyo Institute of Technology, Tokyo, Japan.

Penrose, R. (2007) "The Road to Reality: A Complete Guide to the Laws of the Universe," Vintage

Plato (2000) "The Republic" Translated by Tom Griffith Cambridge, University Press

Plato, "The Symposium," Translated by Benjamin Jowett

Plato, "The Symposium," volume II, Translated by R.E. Alien; Yale University Press

Plato "Cratylus"

Plato (1982) "Parmenides" Translated by Benjamin Jowett; Oxford University

Rousseau, JJ. (1889) "Emile; or Concerning Education," Translated by Eleanor Worthington; Heath & Company-Boston

Rousseau, JJ. (1762) "Emile ou de l'Education," Livre I, II et III; Edition électronique; Chicoutimi-Québec

Sartre, J. (1956) "Being and Nothingness," Hazel E. Barnes' Translation; University of Colorado

Sartre, J. (1946) "L'Existentialisme est un Humanisme," Les Editions Nagel

Sartre, J. (1943) "L'Être et le Néant: Essai D'Ontologie Phénoménologique," Editions Gallimard-Paris

Schopenhauer, A. (1851) "On Women," from Essays of Schopenhauer; the project Gutenberg e-book

Schopenhauer, A. (2004) "Essays of Schopenhauer," The Project Gutenberg E-book of Essays

Schopenhauer, A. (1969) "The World as Will and Representation," Dover Publications

Schopenhauer, A. (2012) "The World as Will and Idea," Translated by R. Haldane and J. Kemp; Vol III. Sixth Edition, Trubner & Co. London

Schrodinger, E. (1944) "What is Life?" Trinity College, Dublin; Chapter 6: Order, Disorder, and Entropy

Smith, N. (1983) "Plato and Aristotle on the Nature of Women," Journal of the History of Philosophy

Tertullian (1890) "The Apology of Tertullian for the Christians," Translated by T. H. Bindley, Merton College, Oxford.

The Holy Bible, King James Version, Genesis 2:7; Leviticus 17:11; 2 Corinthians 5; Job32:8; Jeremiah 31:31-34; 2Corinthinas4:16; Revelation12:7-13; Ezekiel 28; Isaiah 14:12-14;

Tucker, J. (2005) "Life Before Life: A Scientific Investigation of Children's Memories of Previous Lives," St Martin's Press

Tucker, J. (2016) "The Case of James Leininger: An American Case of the Reincarnation Type," Elsevier

Voltaire (1759) "Candide, ou L'Optimisme," Cramer, Geneva

WHO (2017) "Depression and Other Common Mental Disorders: Global Health Estimates," https://apps.who.int/iris/bitstream/handle/10665/254610/WHO-MSD-MER-2017.2-eng.pdf

Wollstonecraft, M. (1792) "A Vindication of the Right of Woman with Strictures on Political and Moral Subject"

Zanou, A. (2021) "The Case Against Sleep: Which One Between the Circadian Clock and Entropy Governs our Sleep Patterns?" Social Science Research Network [Elsevier]

Zanou, A. (2021) "The Mystery of Sleep: The Untold Case of Rest" Social Science Research Network [Elsevier]

Zanou, A. (2021) "Why Do Women Experience Dissociation When Facing Sexual Aggression and Rape?" Social Science Research Network [Elsevier]

Zanou, A. (2022) "On Morality?" Social Science Research Network [Elsevier]

Zanou, A. (2022) "What is Philosophy, and is There Something Called African Philosophy?" Social Science Research Network [Elsevier]

Zanou, D. (2019) "Of Human Spirit, Mind and Soul" Stratton Press

Zanou, D. (2020) "15 Scientific Papers and Philosophical Essays That Could Compel Scholars to Rethink the World," Stratton Press.

Zanou, D. (2020) "The Social Fabric" Amazon KDP

Zanou, D. (2021) "On Ideology: How the Words We Use to Communicate are Creating Much Trouble in Our Society." Amazon KDP.

Zanou, D. (2021) "Understanding the Higgs Scalar Field: Another name for Consciousness," Amazon KDP

Printed in the United States
by Baker & Taylor Publisher Services